AF209120

Awaken Your Soul
Rise and Shine

Nadine Simmerock

Publish: BoD · Books on Demand GmbH, Überseering 33,
22297 Hamburg, bod@bod.de
Print: Libri Plureos GmbH, Friedensallee 273,
22763 Hamburg
ISBN: 978-3-8192-7748-1

"To remember bad experiences and dwell upon them is an abuse of God's gift to us of memory. Rather one should vow, "I shall use memory only to recall good thoughts and experiences. From this moment I banish from my mind all unpleasant memories. They belong to the mortal being. I am a child of the Spirit. I am going to see, hear, taste, touch, feel, and will everything that is good. I shall take only the good from my life's experiences and shall preserve only the good in my memory." Banish forever the abuse of memory."

Paramahansa Yogananda

Dedication

In loving memory of you, dearest Barbara!
My dear friend, who was always filled with love and constantly tried to encourage people to treat each other with more respect and kindness.
Thank you for dancing now and continuing to spread your love through this book and your immortal soul.
With deep gratitude and love for your companionship on Earth and now from the astral realm!
Now you are once again the angel you have always been!
Love you dearly,
Your Nadine

TABLE OF CONTENTS

Introduction- Rise and Shine 8

The Call of Your Soul 10

The Different Levels of Consciousness of a Person .. 12

    The Divine Core: 12

    The Soul: 13

    The Higher Mind: 15

    The Layout Level: 16

    The Blueprint: 17

    The Mass Collective: 18

    The Individual Level: 19

    The Unconscious Level: 20

    The Consciousness – Physical Mind: 22

    The Shadow Creations: 23

The right to be WONDERFUL and WEALTHY 25

    The Essence of Soul Power 25

    The Birthright of Abundance 25

    The Journey to Unfolding 26

    The Power of Authenticity 26

    The Beauty of Being 26

    The Call 26

My Clairvoyance 31

What My Clairvoyance Means to Me 34

Mediumship- I Love the Souls 35

Leave the Shadow Creations Behind......................... 37

Self-Sabotage and Self-Destruction.......................... 43

Joy or Fear.. 51

The Decision.. 55

The Shift... 57

The Golden Meditation for Connecting with Earth and the Universe: 62

I Bring Luck 64

Letting Go oft he Shadows in Our Lives and Reconnecting with Our Inner Light............................ 67

Changing Your Mindset... 69

No More Deals 72

Welcome to the Magical World of Energies 76

Cord Cutting 78

Releasing Foreign Energies.................................... 81

The Golden Canvas – For Releasing.......................... 86

The Golden Canvas- Learn to Manifest 89

Calling Upon Divine Order, Divine Justice and Divine Restoration 96

Your Golden Timeline.. 99

The 12 Soul Levels... 102

Your Soul Essence 115

The Magic of Released Soul Essence........................ *125*

Be a Leader.. *130*

Acknowledgment *132*

Introduction- Rise and Shine

In a world often shaped by hustle and external expectations, we secretly long for deeper meaning, for a life that reflects our heart's truth. *"Awaken Your Soul"* takes you on a transformative journey that has the potential to illuminate and enrich every aspect of your life. This book is an invitation to pause and hear the quiet yet persistent call of your soul. It encourages you to dive into your higher states of consciousness, unfold hidden potentials, and discover the unique power that resides within you.

You will be inspired to let go of old patterns, free yourself from chains, and find the courage to walk your authentic path with confidence and passion.

Together, let's break free from the comfort zone that hold us back and create a space where heart and soul dance in harmony – where you can bloom into the best version of yourself.

"Awaken Your Soul" is not just a book, but an awakening to a life full of meaning, fulfillment, and limitless potential.

Ready to unfold your soul's power?

Then let's get started, and I'll take you on a journey to your soul! With every page you read, you awaken your soul parts again, and more and more will join, until you are the soul once again. With all that belongs to you, your soul path, and your activated soul plan!

I hope that my book will be a beautiful source of inspiration and joy for you, capturing ease and joy in harmony with the soul, and never letting go of it!

To recap briefly, we live in a world where we are often driven by to-do lists and external obligations, and most people long for moments of ease and true joy – those precious moments when the soul breathes and the heart dances with happiness. This joy is not fleeting or dependent on external factors; it springs from deep within you, from the connection with your true essence.

"Awaken Your Soul" invites you to integrate this joy into your life permanently. By freeing yourself from old burdens and leaving

behind the constraints of daily life, you create space for your soul to shine in its full splendor. In this state of lightness, life becomes easier, more graceful, and abundant.

Through conscious mindfulness and the intentional pursuit of inner peace, even everyday challenges become opportunities to recognize and nurture the radiant light within you. With each step in this direction, your path becomes clearer and more joyful, carried by the energy of the heart.

Let's embark on this journey to rediscover the soul in its purest essence and form, and create a world where joy becomes the driving force. For in joy and enthusiasm lies the true magic of life – and it is open to all of us.

May this book encourage you to fully embrace your life, to live each day with enthusiasm, to be excited about yourself, your being, every moment. That is soul power! And it is this unique strength and beauty of your soul that I want to uncover with you!

I hope that every word you read rises into your heart, helping you discover your true magic and recognize the radiant beauty of your own soul.

Thank you.

Rise and shine, and become the best version of yourself, living with enthusiasm!

With love,
Your Nadine

The Call of Your Soul

Do you know the call for more?
The call of the soul when you feel that you're no longer satisfied, a longing for change, renewal, to rise higher, yearning for more, to create something extraordinary, when you feel like you're about to burst, when you know something needs to change? Do you know that feeling?
Then your soul has knocked on your heart's door, and it's time to open it!
There are moments in life when a quiet, yet unmistakable call sounds deep within us – a longing that tells us it's time to leave old paths behind and create new realities. This feeling, that our current environment no longer matches our inner horizons, comes from the soul, inviting us to dream bigger and act bolder.
When the desire for change stirs within you, when you feel your heart longing for something tangible, meaningful, and extraordinary, it is the loving wake-up call of your soul knocking on your heart's door. It reminds you that you are more than what you have lived so far – that within you lies an immeasurable power and creativity waiting to be unleashed.
This inner drive urges you to shed the chains of habit and grow beyond ordinary boundaries. It is an invitation to give space to your heart's energy and blossom in full glory. Your soul longs for you to find your true purpose and have the courage to express your authentic being.
Do not let this call go unheard. Open yourself to the possibilities before you, and trust that your path is guided by your innermost light. For the journey your soul proposes will lead you to a life of fulfillment, truth, and limitless potential.
Then you are not alone, and here and now, you never have to be or feel that way again.
This feeling for MORE is the call of your soul, to be everything you are.
I have heard your call, because you are holding this book in your hands!

Within your soul lies the source of energy, waiting to be discovered, then ignited, to finally be lived.

Never dim your light again, for anything or anyone!

We can only serve the world if we allow our soul's light to fully blossom!

And remember, a desire for more, a heartfelt wish, is always your higher soul, your higher heart, knocking on your soul's door, so you can receive and give even more good!

This book is an invitation to a treasure hunt, YOUR treasure hunt, for the most valuable treasure – your soul.

Connect with your true essence and become a powerful creator of your own reality.

Oh yes, let's begin.

The Different Levels of Consciousness of a Person

Let's dive right in. I want to describe to you the different levels of consciousness that shape our existence:

At the heights of our existence, there is a multifaceted field of levels of consciousness available to us here on Earth, from which we have originated and that shape and influence us in return. Understanding these levels opens up a powerful tool for us to consciously shape our lives and tap into our full potential.

Up here, everything is already given to you, up here everything is taken care of and prepared. Don't believe it? Just wait and see!

It's so important to me that you understand these levels, because once you've understood how you are structured, and it becomes clear to you, when you fully internalize it, no one will ever be able to sell you anything else, trick you, or try to lead you astray. You are the most beautiful being there is, and we will unfold that! I will explain every level available to us, from the highest realms down to the body. I know, the scales will fall from your eyes, lights will turn on, and especially these levels. Just by reading, they will be activated again, and you will simply feel it.

You will feel the truth about yourself!

Let's dive right in:

The Divine Core:

At the highest point is the concept of the **Higher Soul**, the divine core. It rests in divine energy, in God, and can never be attacked or wounded. This is impossible. With this, we are eternally connected to the universal source. It holds all divine knowledge and wisdom within it, reminding us that we are absolute divine beings. Within this lies the so-called Higher Heart, which is in turn connected to the human heart and the cosmic heart, the divine mother.

Invulnerable, untouchable. Do you understand? In truth, nothing can ever happen to us; we are, in truth, untouchable! With this, you are already provided with EVERYTHING you can imagine. Your heart is already connected to the Higher Heart and thus to the cosmic heart. It beats in perfect love. It truly is all one, everything beats in the rhythm of the universe, and you are endlessly nourished by it. The golden light is your pulse, your nourishment, your life energy—everything at once. For you, from this highest source, everything is provided, and it never runs out! Isn't that wonderful?

Here, the statement is emphasized: You are one with God. Yes, you truly are!

Now, I would like to give you a small exercise to activate your connection right away, or if you are truly concerned about someone, because they are not well or perhaps going down a path of self-destruction, and it might seem like they've lost their heart. You can immediately address this level.

Speak to your Higher Soul, the Higher Heart of yourself or the person you are concerned about.

Say: (For another person, please change to "she" or "he")
"Please, my dear Higher Soul and my beloved Higher Heart. You pulse endlessly for me, through all my levels of consciousness, all the way down into my being and into my heart. Please activate healing within me and allow my heart to take up the healthy rhythm from you, dear Higher Heart, and thereby also from the cosmic heart. All the golden, cosmic, divine love pulses within me, and healing begins! Thank you so much!"

Then let go, with deep gratitude and openness to miracles!
The Higher Soul contains everything, it is limitless and almighty!

The Soul:
Below the Higher Soul lies the **soul** itself, our most unique and unmistakable essence, which shapes our deepest drive and inner desires. It carries the knowledge and wisdom of all the experiences our soul has ever had, and gently guides us toward our destiny. Here, you find individuality—the individual spirit. For example, in a

mediumship reading, I can recognize the characteristics of the soul, allowing us to know who is present.

Otherwise, the soul is the pure divine light of the Higher Soul. There is actually no difference, except that here your essence of individuality is added. Your soul shines in pink, gold, and white. And then, through individuality, your soul fragments come into play, waiting to be uncovered and, most importantly, to be lived out by us here on Earth.

The soul is also surrounded by 12 soul layers, which serve as additional protection. They reflect the core values of a soul, or a person. These 12 soul values are our birthright.

They are as follows:
1) Soul Dignity
2) Soul Joy
3) Soul Love
4) Soul Development
5) Soul Intuition
6) Soul Grace
7) Soul Humility
8) Soul Peace
9) Soul Justice
10) Soul Loyalty
11) Soul Abundance
12) Soul Protection

I will explain them in detail in a later chapter.

Here is a small exercise to activate your soul fragments and the 12 soul layers.

Say:

"My dearest soul, you are so wonderful and breathtakingly beautiful. All my 12 soul layers and soul fragments are already available to me, and I ask you to activate them now, for the greatest good and benefit of myself and all beings. Breathe your soul breath through all my layers and fragments, so that they begin to pulse again. They open up, breathe once more. I now take deep breaths as this little human child, and they unite with your soul breath, becoming huge breaths within my soul layers, awakening all my soul fragments and all my levels of consciousness, in perfect harmony with my Higher Soul and my Higher Heart! Thank you so much."

The Higher Mind:
The **Higher Mind** acts as a mediator between our soul and our conscious mind. It provides insights and intuitions that encourage us to look beyond the obvious horizons, to recognize new possibilities, and most importantly, to realize that we are soul!
Our Higher Mind can be thought of as sitting at the peak of a mountain, in alignment with the Higher Soul and the soul, overseeing everything. It sees everything at once, in all directions, and across all timelines. It knows exactly which timeline is the best for you, the highest soul path you can walk. Are you ready to accept it and activate your highest soul plan? This exists on this level, where the soul plan, timelines, and soul path are available to us! Incredible, right?
It's all so exciting and wonderful, isn't it? Everything is here, everything is prepared for us!
The Higher Mind should be completely connected to our physical mind, our consciousness. The two should form a deep friendship, have fluid communication, and work in close collaboration. The Higher Mind is so wonderful, so special, and it's just waiting for you to reconnect with it, to let it act through you, and thereby activate only your consciousness, your timelines, your soul path, and your soul plan! The Higher Mind is the voice of our soul, which constantly and lovingly speaks to us.
Would you like to activate it a little right now?

Then say:
"Dear Higher Mind, I love you and thank you for being here, for always watching over me, even though I wasn't aware of your infinite help and care until now! But now I am, and I am infinitely grateful. Please activate now, through your infinite love for me, the direct

15

connection to my wonderful consciousness, which has been waiting only for your loving friendship. Activate my timelines, my exquisite soul path, and ignite a fireworks display in the activation of my highest, golden soul plan! Everything pulses in your perfection, I can hardly believe how beautiful I am through you. You give me your radiant wisdom, beauty, and connect with my consciousness through intuition. It is an honor that you can work through me on this Earth! Thank you!"

Now, the Higher Mind level splits into two levels.

The Layout Level:
This is your level of manifestation, where you can create and manifest anything! This level is the space between the visible and the invisible. It's where the invisible becomes visible and is then brought into full visibility on Earth! Here, at this level, you have a golden canvas that you can use again to direct your energy and truly create what you desire. You are a wonderful energetic architect, capable of building and creating anything you want! Anything is possible here. You can use your entire creative power to make the invisible visible. For this, I created the seminar "Aura Architecture," so you can learn it in a focused way!
The Higher Mind has a direct influence on this level, so when you manifest something, do it at this level, always in alignment with your Higher Mind—he is your leader, your protector, your magician, your seer—I always say to him: *You are my everything!*
Would you like to use your golden canvas again?

Say:
"I call upon my golden canvas once again into existence. Now I see you before me, huge and golden. You are nourished by the golden ray of Mother Earth and the golden ray of the Universe. Everything I create upon you will become reality, everything you touch turns to gold. I love you, my golden canvas, and here and now, I set my first manifestation upon you, in harmony with my Higher Mind and my

Over-Soul.
Now, set your true soul desire upon it, in the form of a clear image or a movie that plays again and again before you.
Jump into your canvas now and feel how everything pulses, filled with your joy, the gold, and all your belief in it. Feel yourself, feel the joy, the radiance, the pulsing, the fulfillment. No doubt, it is!
Then, jump out of the canvas again, but because you've filled it with you and your being, it lives, and all consciousness levels are now working with you to make it a reality.
It is now a reality!
Thank you!"

The Blueprint:
The term "Blueprint" is often used in connection with a detailed plan or template to create or design something. In your Blueprint level, you have everything you've ever accomplished or created. Your personal development steps, serving as a guide that includes clear steps and strategies to achieve specific goals in this life.
The Blueprint is about unfolding your path that you set for yourself before birth, based on your unique abilities, experiences, and interests. It helps you walk your highest soul path and assists you in transforming your passions into a successful and fulfilling life. The Blueprint serves as a compass, guiding you forward and helping you overcome obstacles while shaping the way to your dream life.
Isn't that wonderful?

Say to yourself:
"Dearest Blueprint level, within you is all my goodness already present, all the magic, all the wonders, all the enchantment. I ask you now to reignite yourself. I do not have to desperately search on Earth, this is becoming crystal clear to me right now. I am allowed to awaken you fully once again with the gold of the Universe, with the love of my Over Soul, and with the passion of my Higher Mind, spreading my arms and expecting miracles! Everything is already

here and is being activated here and now.
Thank you."

The Mass Collective:
In the community of our kind exists the **Mass Collective**, a shared space of consciousness that connects us, and from which we both give and receive. Here, collective experiences and lessons flow, which we can integrate into our individual perception.
The Mass Collective connects all souls that are currently on Earth, and we have agreed to be here with all these souls at this time.
Here, the current rules and forms of life exist, so please do yourself a favor and don't go against everything, draining your own energy. Just an example: WLAN or Wi-Fi, it is unhealthy. Yes. There are so many frequencies; I'm sure one could have found frequencies that wouldn't harm humans. But it is what it is. Can we rebel against it? Of course. Does it help? No.
And that means the Mass Collective. Accept it. It's much more sensible to find a way to protect your body, your being, and your aura, to live in the collective that has already long ago decided that WIFI and these things exist at this time.
Here you find the rules of the world for all humans who are here at this moment.
Do you understand?
Don't waste your precious time fighting against it. Instead, create something beautiful for the Mass Collective!

Say:
"Thank you, dear Mass Collective, for your unstoppable love, in which you are available to all of us souls who are on this Earth at this moment, connecting us and always offering the highest path. I am ready now. I stand before you as a helper and instrument, so that you can work through me here on Earth. I am your golden tool.
I am ready. Thank you!"

The Individual Level:
At the **individual level**, we define our personal identity and self-image. You agreed to be here, in this moment. You chose life on Earth and prepared everything for yourself. Everything. You decided long before to live this life.

At this level, we also find all unresolved karma, meaning everything that is not yet healed and needs to be brought back to peace. Situations, events, past shocks, etc., even with other people. This is where true karma or unresolved issues reside, and it is here where they are seen, recognized, and can be resolved, forgotten, and forgiven.

If you feel stuck in a never-ending loop, where you are continuously told, "You still need to resolve this here, and here, and there, and there's a connection here, and that...," you should step out, because both you and/or the person trying to help you may be stuck in shadow creations.

Once you start digging in the mud there, only more mud will surface, and an endless loop of endlessly resolving karma, past lives, pain, etc., begins, where you never reach a solution. It becomes a never-ending process of resolving endless shadow creations!

Don't put yourself through that anymore, because it's absolutely WRONG! You won't find karma or unresolved issues in shadow creations—they are illusions.

At your individual soul level, you may find something, resolve it, and move forward beautifully and brightly. Do you understand?

This is your very individual level, where everything you have ever been and are is stored. Absolutely everything is here. This is also where the Akashic records and your magical soul star reside. It holds everything about you, it shines, and it always tries to show you the way.

And the beauty is, I think, you have already prepared. You've already stored all the tools here, all the knowledge, and all the wisdom you need to deal with karma or any current challenges. Isn't that genius? Aren't you genius?

You have already set aside all the good and helpful things for yourself, even before you came to Earth.

Say to yourself now:
"I am no longer willing, from this day forward, to voluntarily search for solutions in earthly shadow creations!
From today, I understand that if there is anything unresolved, no matter from which time, for whatever reason, whether caused by me or by another person, I will go to this level and ask for resolution and the appropriate tool, because it is already available to me. At the same time, I forgive, and I know I am forgiven.
Now, I ask for the activation of my Soul Star – so that it may guide and lead me again. Please allow my Akashic Record to shine brightly, for it holds only good things for me.
I remember everything I have made available to myself, and I am grateful for it!
It is that simple! Thank you!"

The Unconscious Level:
Now, we come to the **unconscious level**, where deeply ingrained patterns and imprints reside. Often hidden, they strongly influence our actions and decisions. Our thoughts, beliefs, feelings, and behaviors manifest here, playing a crucial role in shaping our lives. The unconscious holds all the inherited patterns, family programs, ancestral issues, and, of course, childhood imprints. It is in this level that we find the subconscious programming that impacts how we view ourselves, the world, and others.
On this level, our triangle is made up of feelings (heart), thoughts (mind), and actions (body). Ideally, these should form a balanced triangle, and thus a balanced team within us that works for us — in thought power, emotional equilibrium, and positive behavior. The more balanced and positive this interplay is within us, the more balanced we are, and the more harmonious our life becomes. I believe this is where we also find our resilience and whether we are brave enough to move forward.
I find this unconscious level extremely important because this is where the ego is formed.
When everything is balanced, you possess a positive ego. This

means you can set healthy boundaries, are empathetic, honest, healthy, powerful, and you live for both yourself and the greater good.

If the triangle is not balanced, a negative ego arises, leading to selfishness, a lack of empathy, criticalness, fear, anger, and ultimately focusing only on oneself and falling into shadow creations, which then seem very attractive!

For me, one thing is clear: we never get rid of the so-called ego. But why should we? In a positive state, it serves us. It emphasizes our individuality and strength. The issue is that the ego is often seen as negative. Instead of rejecting it, we should celebrate our independence and individual expression here. You just need to have your team on your side.

In the unconscious level resides YOUR team — all the stored beliefs, programs, emotions, and thought processes that should form your team. They should act like cheerleaders, cheering you on, encouraging you, and always being there for you.

They should be shouting: "You are amazing!", "You can do it!", "You are successful!", "I love you!", and so on.

If this level holds wrong programming, it's as if your team, which should be supporting you, is working AGAINST you. In that case, it's time to replace some team members or build a new team.

But again, everything that's wrongfully programmed inside of you can be found here, not in the shadow creations, in the mud, where you may never find your way out. If you resolve and reprogram here, there is an end to it, because once all your team members are working for you, you have a cheerleader team that will be with you forever!

Are you ready for your transformation?

Then say to yourself:
"Dear Triangle, thank you for being here. I am now ready to balance everything that needs balance in my feelings, in my thoughts, in my actions. I am here and today ready to let go of everything old and no longer serving me. All programming from the past, whether from my childhood, from my parents, from family imprints, unresolved

ancestral entanglements, from the here and now, or from past lives, times, planes, or dimensions. Whether it was implanted or I voluntarily took it on. I now ask the gold of this wonderful level to process, transform, and heal everything that is possible at this moment. I am now forming a wonderful cheerleader team that supports, cheers, encourages, and uplifts me.
I am grateful for my individual expression!"

The Consciousness – Physical Mind:

Now we move from the subconscious to the conscious mind!
Our consciousness is the level we experience most directly, as it is connected to the body through the mental mind. Here, external stimuli meet internal reactions, and we decide how to respond to the world around us. This conscious experience allows us to actively shape reality and evolve further.

As mentioned earlier, this level should be in deep friendship with the Higher Mind. This way, we are guided and led through our feelings (intuition) and thoughts (insights), enabling us to make the right decisions and act positively for our highest soul path!

You can imagine that everything that belongs to us in terms of aura, torus field, diamond field, chakras, clairvoyant channels, sensory organs, and the body is part of this level.

The aura is the energy surrounding us; it is us. Surrounding the aura is the so-called diamond field, an indestructible energy field that protects us and connects us with our soul essence. On the outermost layer is the torus field, a self-regenerating energy field around us. Every plant has a torus field, every stone, every apple, every animal, and even the Earth itself.

Everything has energy, and it's so important to recognize that. Even at this level, we've prepared everything good for ourselves. One could almost say we're never alone. In the body, we have the chakras, the clairvoyant channels, sensory perceptions, and so on. Everything is a symphony, a flowing together of all energies.

You are a beautiful composition of various spheres and energy frequencies. You have many helpers by your side, and not to forget, everything you have prepared to safely walk your soul's path!

Say to yourself:
"I thank you, dear consciousness level, for your tireless help. All the gold now flows into my torus field, my diamond field, filling my entire aura, my body, and of course my physical mind, my chakras, my spine, DNA, all organs, brain and brain nerves, and especially it fills my foot chakra and higher self chakra, which support my torus field. I am a wonderful symphony of interwoven frequencies, both physical and subtle.
Thank you!"

The Shadow Creations:
Now, let's move on to the shadow level! The level of **shadow creation** actually isn't in our field, it doesn't even belong to us. It's not a divine level that's specially there for us. It is the self-generated energy field of the inhabitants of the Earth. It becomes a reality when we feel separated from the higher levels; that's when the shadow creations of this world become reality. This means everything becomes a danger, there is chaos, drama, fear, pain, suffering, hatred, anger, power, manipulation, abuse, and death.
This is the mirror image of the world, of humanity, of opposites, of impermanence. If you dig in the mud here, you'll only find more mud. That means, if you're down here and always think, "Oh, now I have to resolve something, I have to recognize something, a person looked at me wrong, I need to find some karma, a bad side of myself..." then you'll never stop because in the mud of shadow creations, there's only mud. You will always find someone down here who wants to hurt you, who isn't honest, who still abuses or cheats. It only has anything to do with you as long as you don't realize that this is not your energy level, not your consciousness level. Recognize that this is truly not you. This is what the visible world tries to make

23

from the invisible world, because down here, you can create shadows so well, monsters, hell.

Do you understand that it has nothing to do with us, it's not contained in our energy field, it comes to life the moment we're born into this world?

These are the creations of thoughts, emotions, feelings, belief in the body, in the physical nature of a person, of humans.

In this energy, you shrink, you become small and fragile.

But only as long as you believe in it. Once you realize who you really are, this shadow world shrinks considerably.

In the shadow creations, you feel trapped, like in an endless loop, waiting a lifetime for everything to get better. Enduring, holding on, and waiting are the basic energies there. Do you really want that?

But if you have the understanding of these true consciousness levels, this knowledge empowers you to lead a life full of clarity, connection to God, and meaning because you live your soul, your highest being!

Wow, this is so brilliant. You are brilliant, you have everything you need to unfold your soul!

This knowledge gives you the most important tool: the ability to consciously choose and design your own journey in alignment with your true soul being.

With this knowledge, you regain your power!
Congratulations.
You are a creative, wonderful being, and when you uncover that once more, miracles happen!
Your magical power explodes, and you shine because you are YOU!

The right to be WONDERFUL and WEALTHY

You now know exactly what a wonderful and wealthy soul you are. You are an incredible source of creation, your energy is limitless, and the thinking energy substance of the universe is waiting for you to use it and shape it.

I love every single soul, I love the beauty of every individual person. I have always used my gift to help people unfold their soul's beauty again. My soul's calling has always been to awaken the soul of a person. My love is so vast because when you free yourself again, you can become a leader in this world, a healed leader, ready to create something much greater than just for yourself.

From today, always go upwards, into all the wonderful consciousness levels available to you, but never again into the shadow creations.

Your wonderful energy is too valuable to direct it into the negative field, making yourself feel small and worthless.

You possess the soul power and the birthright to live your own beauty!

The Essence of Soul Power

Our soul power is the source of our creativity, courage, and inner guidance. It reflects our values, dreams, and the unique gifts we are meant to share with the world. When we step into our soul power, we recognize our uniqueness and begin to view life from a perspective of possibilities rather than limitations.

The Birthright of Abundance

From birth, we all have the right to live a life of wealth and abundance – in every way. This abundance goes beyond material prosperity; it includes emotional, mental, and spiritual fulfillment. A life of abundance means living in harmony with oneself and one's surroundings. It means shaping relationships, career, and everyday experiences that align with our inner truth.

The Journey to Unfolding

Stepping into our full soul power is a journey that requires courage and devotion, igniting self-love. It begins with the conscious decision to explore our own truth and remove the masks we've worn out of fear or conformity. This journey requires us to meet ourselves with self-compassion, self-love, and acceptance while freeing ourselves from old beliefs and self-doubt.

The Power of Authenticity

A life in authentic soul power means aligning our thoughts, words, and actions. It means being honest with ourselves and others, even when the path seems rocky. Through authenticity, we inspire not only ourselves but also those around us to live their own truth and discover their personal beauty.

The Beauty of Being

When we reside in our soul power, our inner beauty blossoms—a beauty that grows from self-love, true fulfillment, and inner peace. This radiant presence attracts like-minded individuals, opportunities, open doors, and experiences that align with our highest vision of ourselves.

The Call

Let us proudly embrace this birthright. Let us step into the power of our soul by sharing our unique talents and passions with the world. Let us be guided by the vision of a life that sparkles with beauty, wealth, and meaning. The possibility to fully live this beauty is present in every moment and in every decision we make. Remember, the key is already within you. You are entitled to claim your full soul power and enrich this world with your radiant light.

I have been clairvoyant since birth. My world consists primarily of energies, and I know that in the universe, all around us, at all times and in every moment, there is a thinking substance—an energy from which everything is created. Every soul is a piece of heaven that has come to Earth, but most often, it forgets its extraordinary power and dresses itself anew each time to play a new role. We don't just clothe ourselves with a body and then with garments; we also take on identities—whether male or female, professions, nationalities, and more.

But each of us carries a unique gift within, a gift meant for this world! Imagine if you were to remove all these layers and stand there as nothing but your piece of heaven—your soul. Then, you would finally share this gift with the world!

In truth, this piece of heaven is, of course, the soul. It is always present—we just need to let it shine again beneath all the layers of shadow clothing.

For me, it is an honor to be clairvoyant, and I always strive to explain things as clearly and simply as possible—to "bring them down to Earth," to make them practical and understandable for everyone.

The laws of the universe are simple, as you now know. They are not complicated. Anything that appears complicated, anything that makes you believe you must struggle endlessly, dig through the mud, or do everything alone—set it aside immediately. Any concept that confuses you deeply originates from the shadow creations.

Everything else is simple!

In the previous chapter on the different levels of consciousness, you internalized this truth. You have seen that you are taken care of. Shift your attention upwards—you are supported, you are guided, everything is easy, you have prepared well, and your Oversoul carries you.

YOU are a creative being!

Your own thought is a creative power! A thought you hold onto can create anything because it shapes the formless substance of the universe on your golden canvas and brings it to Earth.

It is completely wrong to believe in poverty—because that is one of the shadow creations! YOU are the most WONDERFUL and RICHEST being in this universe. Do you see that?

In this book, I will show you how to use your creative energy—in the simplest, most straightforward way, yet with the highest efficiency. In fact, you have already begun.

The universe is not complicated or confusing! No, it is beautiful, golden, and abundant.

Since I can see energies, I know one thing for certain—nothing ever stands still. The entire universe is filled with movement, and everything strives for GROWTH, EXPANSION, and RENEWAL!

That means YOU have a right to constant evolution, a right to use your full power, to show your beauty, and to enjoy the wealth you already possess. From today onward, you unfold upward, you blossom upward, you are from above.

You should never settle for less—especially not for shadow creations! You are an extraordinary being in this universe, with unlimited positive power, love, beauty, elegance, energy, and wealth. Put negativity aside. Release false thoughts and emotions—especially those that are stagnant, fearful, or filled with anger.

Again, ALL of these- ALL are shadow creations.

You are not dependent on anyone or inferior to anyone—not even a government. Of course, I could focus on all the negativity—on every bad news report, on television, on what politicians, governments, big corporations, the pharmaceutical industry, and advertisements are doing wrong or how they manipulate you. But if you do that, you enter the shadow creations. All of these are tools of shadow creations on Earth.

Yes, politics creates tension, the media manipulates, and the advertising industry knows exactly what it is doing!

Speaking of advertising, let's take a moment to explore how it works. What Happens When You Watch an Advertisement?

First, advertisers know that our emotions are in the driver's seat. Your emotions move you, so they use them against you.

They also know that if an advertisement only remains in your conscious mind, it won't have the same effect as when it enters your subconscious mind.

Your conscious mind has the power to choose—to decide whether you actually need something or not. Do I want to take in this information or not?

Do you know the terms inductive and deductive?

Your conscious mind is inductive—meaning it chooses what to let into your subconscious and what to reject.

Your subconscious mind, however, is deductive—it only accepts what it is given. It cannot choose, but it has your incredible Cheerleader Team inside.

Your subconscious relies on your conscious mind to be wise and allow in only the best.

So, what does advertising do?

It tricks your conscious mind through emotions. It bypasses your natural inductive barrier, and suddenly, the advertisement is working directly within your subconscious!

And just like that, you need everything they want you to need.

You're probably wondering: How exactly do they trick your natural protection barrier?

Through these three emotions:
- Fascination
- Shock
- Agreement

Exactly at the moment when you are startled in a movie, deeply immersed in feelings of love, or crying along—when you are highly emotional—advertisements are inserted, and suggestion takes place.

This happens on YouTube and other platforms. Pay attention and observe it carefully!

Do not allow yourself to be hypnotized anymore and thereby be driven into mental poverty, keeping you focused on all these shadow creations.

You are one of the most WONDERFUL and RICHEST beings. It breaks my heart to see how many people remain dormant, trapped in shadow energy, waiting for something to happen or for someone to save them.

In the shadow creations, waiting and enduring are key characteristics, because down there, you are not capable of creating or manifesting.

From a young age, I have always wanted one thing: for every single person to step into their full potential, to share their beauty, strength, energy, and love with this world.

YOU ARE THE SOUL! You are the richest being that exists.

If you truly follow the fundamentals in this book, you will become one of the richest beings—both internally and externally. There is absolutely nothing wrong with being RICH! The entire universe is RICH!

It is filled with magical beauty, abundance, renewal, love, joy, and gratitude! And so are YOU—you are a reflection of all of this!

Reclaim your birthright.

It is your birthright! That's how it is, and nothing else. Rise up!

The truth is:

You are the soul and you have a body.

You are the most WONDERFUL and RICHEST being because you are a soul, and you possess the creative power that you can express through your mind and body.

Step into the higher fields available to you and stop waiting—start creating!

You are the creator of your life!

My Clairvoyance

I want to take this moment to share my deep gratitude with you—gratitude for a gift that was given to me and has enriched my life in such miraculous ways. A gift that I now hope to give back to you: my clairvoyance.

This gift has always opened the energetic world to me. As you now see, it is a world filled with these wonderful levels of consciousness, full of love, insights, perspectives, and connections that go beyond the obvious. Clairvoyance allows me not only to recognize the hidden facets of life but also to see with a depth that extends far beyond the physical.

I feel infinitely blessed to have this gift in my life, and that is why sharing it has always been my highest priority—communicating what I see. Not only through my aura readings or angel readings, but above all, by showing how each individual can reclaim their own power. My clairvoyance is my compass, always guiding me toward inner growth, understanding, love, and compassion. It brings clarity in all areas of life and provides guidance. But most importantly, it allows me to support and inspire you on your unique journey.

In a world where uncertainty and challenges have become ever-present, I see it as my sacred duty to use this gift to bring light into unknown paths. That is why it is so close to my heart to share this space of possibilities with you, so that together, we can experience trust and an unstoppable spirit.

May this gift of clairvoyance, like a gentle beam of light, always illuminate the path—not only for me but especially for you and for all people. My dear readers, I thank you for being part of this journey and for allowing me to contribute, in my own way, to your life.

I have never known the world any other way, but I am aware that clairvoyance is still far from being widely accepted in society. Nevertheless, I am deeply grateful for this ability, which enables me every day to recognize the hidden treasures of the soul and the universe in each person and to fully unveil the soul's essence.

With every glimpse into the invisible realms, I feel a profound connection to creation and an immeasurable gratitude for this unique gift. I invite you to travel into your soul through this book and to discover the wonders that lie beyond the visible. May my clairvoyance inspire and touch you as we explore together the magic and beauty of the unseen. And most importantly—know that you carry this gift within you as well.

You have a third eye—it only needs to be activated.

Let's take a brief look at both the scientific and spiritual perspectives!

Scientific Explanation:

From a scientific perspective, clairvoyance is often seen as a phenomenon that lies outside conventional understanding. It has not yet been fully explained or accepted by mainstream science.

However, some theories suggest that clairvoyance may be related to the brain's ability to access and interpret information beyond the five traditional senses. One hypothesis proposes that clairvoyance could be linked to the brain's ability to process subtle energy fields or electromagnetic frequencies that are not typically detected by our ordinary senses.

It is believed that some individuals possess an increased sensitivity or an innate ability to perceive and interpret these energies, allowing them to gain insights and information that others may not access as easily. While scientific research on clairvoyance is still ongoing, it is important to note that the scientific community has not yet reached a consensus on its existence or mechanisms.

Nonetheless, many people continue to report personal experiences that they attribute to clairvoyant abilities.

Spiritual Explanation:

From a spiritual perspective, clairvoyance is often regarded as an intuitive or psychic ability that transcends the physical senses. It is believed to involve immersing oneself in higher levels of consciousness, connecting with spiritual energies, and accessing information from the collective consciousness or the spiritual realm.

According to spiritual beliefs, clairvoyance can be seen as an extension of our innate spiritual nature.

It is thought that individuals can develop and enhance their clairvoyant abilities through spiritual practices such as meditation, energy work, or connecting with higher dimensions.

Spiritual explanations often emphasize the idea that clairvoyance is a gift that enables individuals to perceive and interpret subtle energies, symbols, or messages that are not immediately obvious to the ordinary senses. It is considered a means of gaining deeper insights, guidance, and spiritual wisdom—supporting personal growth, healing, and a deeper understanding of one's life path.

It is important to acknowledge that scientific and spiritual perspectives on clairvoyance may differ, and individuals may resonate more with one viewpoint than the other. Ultimately, the interpretation of clairvoyance can vary based on personal beliefs, experiences, and cultural backgrounds.

What My Clairvoyance Means to Me

What does my clairvoyance mean to me? It is far more than just an ability; it is a profound gift from the universe, woven into a great responsibility that I carry with respect and devotion.

From the depths of my heart, I believe that this gift is not a random blessing but a carefully woven part of my existence, calling me to use it for the greater good. Every time I apply my clairvoyance, I feel the gentle yet determined guidance of a higher purpose showing me the way.

My clairvoyance allows me to see into dimensions that often remain hidden, and it encourages me to share these insights with love and compassion—to make them visible for you. I see it as my sacred duty to use this gift for the benefit of all, always with the intention of bringing light into the lives of others, encouraging them, and offering them the space to recognize and embrace their own truth.

The souls whose paths cross mine enrich me just as much as I hope to enrich them. In the connection that arises from this, the true meaning of my work is revealed.

With every aura reading, my dedication deepens, and each time I use my gift, I reaffirm my promise to always apply it with love and truth. In this mission, I not only find fulfillment but also unwavering motivation to continue learning, growing, and serving.

I wake up every day with enthusiasm—to help, to heal, and to love. For this, I am infinitely grateful and remain profoundly humble.

The love for each individual soul is the reflection of every higher soul in the cosmos.

That is why I love. That is why I give. That is why I exist. Love is everything!

Mediumship- I Love the Souls

Welcome tot he World of Mediumship:

I lovingly call my mediumship events *"The Bridge"* because, in that moment, I build a bridge between the physical world and the realm of souls—the astral world. As a medium, I have the privilege of serving as this bridge, facilitating communication between individuals and their departed loved ones. Mediumship is based on the understanding that consciousness continues beyond physical death and that the souls of our loved ones remain present and accessible to us. We do not summon them; they come on their own. Through my abilities, I can perceive and interpret the energies, messages, and presence of these souls. During a mediumship session, I create a safe and sacred space where you can connect with your departed loved ones. Using my intuitive abilities, I establish a link that allows the transmission of messages, validations, and healing. The purpose of mediumship is to offer comfort, closure, forgiveness, and healing to those seeking contact with their loved ones—or to those whom the departed wish to reach. This experience allows people to feel and perceive the presence of their loved ones firsthand. In this moment, hearts open wide as the energy elevates, and individuals begin to experience healing, forgiveness, gratitude, and love. This is the most beautiful moment! It is a magical experience, where beloved souls take us to a completely different level—into the consciousness of the soul, just beneath the Oversoul and the Great Heart. This is where true healing takes place! No words can fully describe the blessing that unfolds during such a reading.

It is important to emphasize that mediumship is not about predicting the future or providing specific outcomes. Instead, it is the sacred moment when two worlds intertwine, when the invisible is made visible through love.

During these sessions, living souls are gently guided to see beyond the tangible, allowing them to experience profound healing. It is a deeply personal and transformative journey that can bring immense healing, closure, and a sense of love and peace.

Through my work, I have learned that a soul always seeks to fill the space left by its departure with light, love, and positive energy. If this does not happen, the void is filled with the grief of those left behind—perpetuating sorrow. But this is not what enlightened souls desire. They understand that lingering in the shadows keeps us unaware of our soul's power, forgetting that we remain connected at all times. Theirs is a message of pure love, blessing, acceptance, and a level of respect beyond human comprehension.

Pure love and blessing.

Leave the Shadow Creations Behind

And here we are, entering the next chapter—the realm of shadow creations and what it truly means to dwell in this lower state. Remaining in this space demands an immense amount of energy. Here, we are so far removed from ourselves that mere survival becomes an exhausting struggle.

To be yourself, to embody your soul, your own light—to simply BE YOURSELF —requires no effort. That is the very source of power within us.

The Shadow Creations and the Return to the Inner Light of the Soul:

In this complex world, we often encounter shadow creations—beliefs and fears born from insecurity, power abuse, competition, scarcity, anger, and the struggles of earthly life. These shadows can deeply influence our thoughts and actions, trapping us in fear and disconnecting us from our true essence. They drain us completely because, first, we are separated from our soul, and second, there is no positive energy source in this state to replenish us.

These illusions—so real, so tangible, so terrifying—stand in contrast to the true nature of our soul, which is made of pure light, love, and infinite joy. The soul knows no fear; it understands only love and expansion. It is the very source that fills us with power and authenticity.

Now is the time to release the illusions of shadow creations. These fear-based beliefs keep us from the abundance that is our birthright and limit our true potential. By freeing ourselves from these shadows, we make space to perceive life from a perspective of love and light.

To return to our inner light, we must seek silence and listen to the voice of our soul. It takes courage to break free from old patterns and refocus on what is real and true. In connection with our inner light, we find the clarity that guides us through the darkest times and strengthens us to see the world with hope and confidence.

I encourage you to read the daily activations of each consciousness level—this will help you focus on where you truly want to direct your energy. And remember, our inner light always shines, even when it is momentarily obscured by shadows. It is an inexhaustible source of renewal and healing. When we focus on this light and allow it to guide us, we begin to recognize the beauty and boundlessness of our own soul.

Let us find the courage to leave these shadow creations behind and embrace the truth of our soul. Only by consciously choosing light and love can we transform our lives and the world around us.

Shadow creations have embedded the cycle of abuse deeply into human consciousness—whether consciously or unconsciously. This cycle includes love bombing, tension, and explosion phases, which have led to a world filled with scarcity, fear, competition, anger, and power abuse. But you know this has nothing to do with your true origin or your authentic being! The energy of competition carries millennia-old programming that separates us from our soul. That is the only truth within it. Scarcity and competition thinking generate destructive emotions, thoughts, behaviors, and actions. That is logical and understandable, right?

The spread of this low-frequency energy—planted through power abuse, manipulation, and the illusion of scarcity—makes people believe in shadow creations. If we experience financial lack, it feels undeniably real. If illness manifests, it is visible and physically felt. But all of these conditions stem from scarcity thinking—the belief in lack—which in turn creates an energetic state of deficiency within your mind, heart, every cell, and energy field. From this scarcity, illnesses, financial loss, unemployment, conflicts, and suffering arise. In shadow creations, lack is overwhelming.

This leads to the belief that we must be faster, higher, and endlessly better than everyone else. People start chasing something, losing themselves in the material world and in the shadows of existence. Here is the golden key that everyone carries with them!

TAKE RESPONSIBILITY FOR YOURSELF.

Here, Now, Today.

Make the decision today to leave these shadow creations behind.

And now, I would love to show you what all this stress does to your chakras—and ultimately, to your body.

What Happens to the Chakras

The concept of chakras, particularly the foot chakras, is deeply rooted in energy and spiritual work.
Chakras are energy centers within the body, and in many spiritual traditions, it is understood that they influence physical, emotional, mental, and spiritual well-being. Here, I want to focus especially on the foot chakras and the Higher Self chakra, as they are crucial and simultaneously connected to the torus field.

In the human body, the torus field is often associated with the energetic field of the heart. It represents how our hearts transmit and receive energetic information, emphasizing our connection to ourselves and our surroundings. The torus field is the self-regenerating and self-healing force within us. This energy flows through us and upwards, passing through the Higher Self chakra, where it opens us to femininity, the power of receiving—ideas, visions, and manifestations. At this stage, the human being radiates outward, existing in complete connection with the universe. The energy then flows down the sides of the body, entering again through the foot chakras as masculine energy—the force of action and implementation. This masculine energy brings the visions and ideas received through the feminine into reality, making them visible and tangible in the world. The energy then continues its cycle, flowing through the body once again and back upward.
This energetic flow does not just surround humans—it encompasses all living beings. Every plant, fruit, vegetable, rock, and even the Earth itself possesses a torus field. We are all interconnected within this universal energy system!
Understanding the torus field helps us become aware of our own energy flow and how it affects our well-being. It is a model that illustrates how we receive, transform, and emit energy, shaping both our personal health and our relationship with the world.
This concept invites us to reflect on the balance and flow of energy in our lives and to embrace the harmony that exists within the greater whole. By aligning ourselves with this universal energy, we step into

a state of balance, creation, and connection—fully rooted in our soul's power.

What Happens When a Person Has No Foot Chakras and Higher Self Chakra:

1. ## Loss of Grounding and Connection:
   - The foot chakras are traditionally responsible for connecting us to the Earth. They help us stay grounded, provide a sense of stability, and support the balance between body and mind. If these chakras are blocked or absent, the sense of grounding can be lost, leading to feelings of disorientation or insecurity. The Higher Self chakra is responsible for connecting us to the universe.
   It helps us feel aligned and safe. Without this connection, a person may collapse inward and perceive shadow creations as real.

2. ## Overactivation of the Root Chakra:
   - The base chakra, also called the root chakra, represents basic needs such as security, survival, money, strength, endurance, and trust. When the foot chakras and Higher Self chakra do not function properly, energy imbalances can arise in the root chakra. This means the person may shift into the shadow realm and start believing in its illusions. As a result, a strong survival energy emerges, leading to a heightened fight mode where nothing feels safe anymore. This survival state can become even more pronounced and manifest in their reality.

3. Invitation of Shadow Creations:

- ◦ Without the balance and stability provided by grounding and universal connection, there is a tendency to focus on fears and insecurities. This often leads to shadow creations—negative beliefs and behaviors driven by a mindset of lack and fear, which then manifest and multiply in one's life.

4. Struggle and Resistance:

- ◦ The lack of grounding flow and universal flow causes a person to fall into a constant state of struggle, energetically fighting against perceived threats instead of being in a state of flow and acceptance. This resistance can create inner stress and tension, as well as conflicts with the external world.

Self-Sabotage and Self-Destruction

Self-sabotage and self-destruction are deeply rooted patterns operating in the shadows of our psyche. They are masters of disguise, often woven unconsciously into our behavior and thinking, manifesting in various ways. As shadow creations, they disguise themselves as defense mechanisms, while in reality, they undermine our most progressive aspirations and well-being—sometimes leading to addictive behaviors or, on a physical level, autoimmune weaknesses or diseases.

These negative patterns often arise from old beliefs formed through past experiences or learned behaviors, convincing us that we are not good enough or that we have been painfully rejected. This can create the deep-seated belief that we do not deserve good things in life. These patterns act like invisible threads, influencing our decisions, blocking our dreams, and trapping us in a seemingly endless cycle of failure.

On a mental level, they lead to negative self-talk and doubt; emotionally, they foster fear and insecurity. Spiritually, they attack our core beliefs, and physically, they can even manifest as autoimmune diseases, subtly causing the immune system to turn against the body.

Self-destruction is an extreme form of self-sabotage, deeply embedded in the subconscious, often triggered by feelings of unworthiness, shame, or unresolved trauma. If left unrecognized and untransformed, these patterns can have significant negative effects on all aspects of life.

Self-sabotage is a subtle yet powerful mechanism that can affect our lives in countless ways. Often deeply ingrained in the subconscious, it causes us to stand in our own way, preventing us from reaching our full potential and achieving our goals. Here are some of the far-reaching consequences of self-sabotage:

Effects of Self-Sabotage

1. **Missed Opportunities:**
   - Self-doubt and negative self-talk often lead to us not recognizing or pursuing opportunities. The fear of failure—or even success—can hold us back, trapping us in an endless cycle shadow creations, of starting and stopping, waiting and enduring.

2. **Lowered Self-Esteem:**
   - Regular patterns of self-sabotage, such as procrastination, gradually erode our confidence. With every missed goal or unfinished project, feelings of inadequacy grow, creating a cycle of shame and disappointment. Shame, guilt, disappointment, and fear are among the "worst" emotions, the ones with the lowest-frequency that drain our energy.

3. **Stagnation in Personal and Professional Growth:**
   - Self-sabotage blocks progress and growth. When we unconsciously create obstacles, we remain stuck in our personal and professional development, unable to move forward.

4. **Health Consequences:**
   - The stress and frustration caused by self-sabotaging tendencies can negatively impact both mental and physical health.
   Chronic stress weakens the immune system and increases the risk of various health issues.

5. **Relationship Issues:**
   - A lack of self-trust can also affect our relationships. Self-sabotage often manifests as unnecessary tests, drama, or conflicts, creating emotional distance and making deeper connections more difficult.

6. **Suppressing the Inner Voice:**
   - When we engage in self-sabotage, we ignore our inner voice—our intuition, the whisper of our heart, soul, and higher mind. This disconnect leads to feelings of disorientation, rejection, and failure, keeping us from aligning with our true desires and purpose.

Self-destruction is a destructive pattern that can be deeply embedded in the subconscious, often triggered by feelings of unworthiness, shame, or unresolved trauma. These patterns represent intense forms of self-sabotage and, if left unrecognized and untransformed, can have significant consequences in all areas of life.

Effects of Self-Destruction

1. **Emotional and Mental Harm:**
   - Self-destructive thoughts fill the mind with negativity and self-loathing, potentially leading to serious mental health struggles such as depression, anxiety, or a persistently low sense of self-worth. This creates a vicious cycle where negative thoughts fuel negative actions, reinforcing an already damaged self-image.

2. Strained Relationships:

- Self-destructive behavior can make interactions with others difficult. It may lead to sabotaging relationships, sowing distrust, or repeatedly engaging in unhealthy relationship patterns.

3. Physical Health Deterioration:

- Harmful habits such as poor nutrition, substance abuse, and neglect of self-care often accompany self-destructive tendencies. Over time, the body may respond with chronic illnesses or health crises resulting from a lack of self-nurturing.

4. Career and Creative Blocks:

- These destructive patterns can stifle creative potential and hinder professional growth. The fear of failure or the belief of being unworthy can cause missed opportunities and stagnation.

5. Spiritual and Personal Disconnection:

- A separation from one's true self and higher values or aspirations can occur, often leading to a sense of aimlessness and disorientation. When inner guidance and joy are blocked, life may feel empty and devoid of meaning.

Ways to Overcome Self-Sabotage and Self-Destruction

To truly step into the abundance and light of our true being, it is essential to consciously leave behind the shadow aspects that keep us trapped. These shadows are not our true selves but rather manifestations of fears and limiting beliefs that cling to negativity and restriction. They are the invisible chains that hold us back, keeping us stuck in old, unhelpful patterns.

The first step toward liberation is recognizing these shadows as illusions that no longer need to define us. They are the fears whispering that we are not good enough, the doubts that keep us small, and the worries that cloud our visions. Yet, all of these are mere illusions, created by past experiences that should hold no power over our present.

Consciously choosing to release these shadow creations is a powerful message—to the universe and to our own hearts—that we are ready to embrace our true selves. By letting go of these limitations, we create space for our inner light to shine, clear and radiant. Beyond the shadows lies the unfolding of our true potential, where we discover our deepest strength and authenticity.

Our true essence is not trapped in darkness; it reaches out to us from the realms of light, filled with hope, joy, and peace. It is an invitation to extend our hand and experience our soul in its most beautiful form. Let us accept this invitation, leave the shadows behind, and consciously step into our own greatness. For it is there, in the light, that we find the life that is rightfully ours in all its fullness.

Overcoming Self-Sabotage:

1. **Increase Self-Awareness:** The first step is recognizing when and how self-sabotage occurs. Journaling and self-reflection can be valuable tools in this process.
2. **Identify Triggers:** Determine what causes self-sabotaging behaviors. Is it fear, perfectionist tendencies, or the worry of not being good enough?
3. **Establish Positive Routines:** Replace self-sabotaging behaviors with healthy and supportive habits that foster personal growth.
4. **Develop Self-Compassion:** Approach yourself with kindness and patience. Acknowledge that these patterns were learned and can be transformed with mindfulness and support.
5. **Visualize Your Goals:** Focus on what you want to achieve and regularly visualize your success. This helps shift attention to positive outcomes.
6. **Seek Support:** Sometimes, professional guidance can help uncover deeper patterns and facilitate meaningful change.

Overcoming Self-Destruction

1. **Create Awareness:** The first step toward transformation is recognizing these patterns and identifying their triggers.
2. **Inner Work:** Addressing the root causes of these patterns, often with therapeutic support, is essential. Integrating shadow aspects and healing past wounds fosters new understanding and self-acceptance.
3. **Healthy Self-Care:** Develop routines that promote well-being. Regular physical activity, a balanced diet, and sufficient sleep are crucial for both physical and mental health.
4. **Positive Relationships:** Surround yourself with people who uplift and support you. Building a strong support system can be key to breaking old patterns.
5. **Mind-Body Practices:** Meditation, yoga, or mindfulness training can help maintain harmony between body and mind, fostering a sense of peace and balance.

6. **Spiritual Practice:** Connecting with a higher power or your spiritual self can provide comfort and guidance on the path to self-healing.

And most importantly, solve the causes.

Self-sabotage, self-destruction, addictions, etc., are not the root causes—they are not the actual problem. These behaviors are attempts at solutions. I am sharing with you once again the small healing prayer, slightly modified, from the individual level—where everything unresolved and karmic can be dissolved! Remember, everything can be resolved—quickly, easily, and permanently. Stop digging through the mud. See that these patterns are not the real problem, but that the root lies much deeper. The actual issue is deeply rooted in the belief that you are not good enough. You have experienced such a painful rejection that it became unbearable—you could hardly bear yourself. Do you understand? Such a deep conviction within you, that you are unworthy, has led you to these behaviors in an attempt to resolve it.

Now, read the prayer calmly. Let it sink in and feel how you dissolve the shadow energy within you.

Say to yourself now:

"From this day forward, I am no longer willing to seek solutions within earthly shadow creations! I also stop sabotaging or even destroying myself out of desperation.

Enough—I am no longer willing to do this.

I refuse to believe that I am bad! I now ask that the magnificent gold of this beautiful realm heals the entire original situation, in all directions of time and for all eternity!

With this, any form of self-sabotage and self-destruction within me is dissolved—no matter from which time, no matter the reason or cause, whether created by me or someone else. I now ask this wonderful realm for the liberation of all these negative behaviors and programs within me, including the original situation. Everything is now permeated by the golden light, and I gratefully receive the necessary tools, as they are already available to me. At the same time, I forgive myself, I forgive everyone else, and I know that I am forgiven.

Now, I ask for the activation of my Soul Star—to guide and lead me once again—of mine Torus Field and my entire aura. Please let my Akashic Records shine, containing only goodness for me. The wonderful, healing gold surrounds me, and I know I can do this!

I remember everything that I have made available to myself, and I rejoice in it!

It's that simple!

Thank you!"

Joy or Fear

Consciousness or Shadow Creations?
I believe you have long understood what this is about and how the truth unfolds. I want to delve a little deeper into the topic of the Foot Chakra and the Higher Self Chakra, as they are incredibly important. When you are connected to your levels of consciousness, I can guarantee that you are living in joy. You will experience life with enthusiasm and savor every moment.
If you are dwelling in the shadow realm, I can guarantee that you are living in fear. You will spend every day trying to avoid fear, using all your energy just to survive.
Imagine everything as frequencies. Everything vibrates at different frequencies—like layers of energy stacked upon each other. Each layer represents a level of consciousness, a vibration, a thought energy. This means you can leave behind a certain frequency if it no longer aligns with you—for example, when you have worked on yourself and profoundly changed your thoughts. With this transformation, your frequency shifts, and you leave behind the old version of yourself, stepping into a new energetic frequency.
So, when you outgrow a particular level of consciousness, you naturally rise above its vibration, energy, and associated thought patterns and emotions. You must leave it behind and will automatically transition to the next level of consciousness.
This is exactly what you are doing right now—you are naturally shifting out of the shadow creations and increasingly stepping into the vibration of your higher being.

At this point, I want to highlight the three deepest, most ingrained fears—so that you can recognize them, release them, and see clearly that they stem entirely from the shadow realm. Again, I will emphasize the Foot Chakra and the Higher Self Chakra, as they play a crucial role in this process.

The 3 Greatest Fears:

1) Fear of Death – Fear of Loss
2) Fear of Life – Fear of Existence
3) Fear of People – Fear of Their Actions and Reactions

These three fears are deeply rooted in the Foot Chakra, as it holds all worldly experiences—including past life memories and karmic imprints.
We can also apply this to the Higher Self Chakra, but here, it's more about the soul and consciousness levels.
At this level, it goes beyond fear—it becomes pure panic, which can completely shut down the entire system when triggered. This energy then explodes, overwhelming and paralyzing us.
Do you know the feeling of panic? The loss of control?

1) The panic of losing the soul – Fear of soul loss
2) The panic of being annihilated – Fear of the soul's destruction
3) The panic of people – Fear of rejection – Fear of exposing the true essence of the soul

Every one of us carries one of these soul-deep fears—a fear so overwhelming that it feels like drowning, like there is no escape. But this only happens when we are still trapped in shadow creations.
Because now you already know: None of this is real.
You cannot lose your soul, and it cannot be destroyed.

To resolve these fears, I have created a deep transformational seminar, **"Awaken Your Soul"** (Find more details on my website: www.nadinesimmerock.com)

Practical Ways to Manage These Fears in Everyday Life:

1. Daily Gratitude Practice:

- **Exercise:** Every morning, write down three things you are grateful for. These can be big or small things that bring you joy. Consciously focusing on the positive aspects of your life helps you start the day with an optimistic mindset.

2. Joy Journal:

- **Exercise:** At the end of the day, note down at least one moment in which you experienced joy. This practice trains your mind to recognize and appreciate happy moments more consciously.

3. Breath & Mindfulness Exercise:

- **Exercise:** Take five minutes daily to focus on your breath. Inhale deeply and exhale slowly. With each exhale, release worries, and with each inhale, open yourself up to new energy. Feel how these mindful moments fill you with joy and inner peace.

4. Active Movement:

- **Exercise:** Engage in a physical activity that brings you joy, such as dancing, yoga, cycling, or walking. Spend at least 20 minutes daily moving. Physical activity releases endorphins, which naturally boost your mood.

5. Visualization of Joy:

- **Exercise:** Find a quiet place, close your eyes, and visualize a moment where you felt pure happiness and alignment with yourself. Relive this moment, embrace the feeling, and allow that positive energy to flow into your present life.

6. Act of Giving:

- **Exercise:** Look for opportunities to bring joy to others—whether through a smile, a kind word, or a small gesture of help. Giving kindness creates happiness both for you and those around you, fostering a sense of fulfillment.

7. Creative Expression:

- **Exercise:** Engage in a creative activity that inspires you—painting, writing, playing music, or crafting. Creativity is a powerful source of joy and helps you reconnect with your inner flow. Let your intuition guide you.

8. Freude-Check-in: Joy Check-in:

- **Exercise:** Set a daily reminder to pause for a moment and check in with yourself: Are you experiencing joy? If not, ask yourself, what small thing could bring you joy right now? Maybe listening to your favorite song, expressing gratitude, or simply taking a deep breath.

By integrating these practices into your daily routine, you will increase your ability to experience joy while naturally shifting your focus away from fear.

The Decision

Making a true decision means choosing consciously—a choice that comes from deep within, in alignment with your values, beliefs, and authentic purpose. It is not influenced by external expectations or fleeting emotions but guided by what feels truly right and harmonious in your heart. A true decision has the power to transform your entire life. Are you ready to make it?

What Does a True Decision Bring?

1. **Clarity and Alignment:**

   ° When you make a decision that aligns with your inner self, you gain clarity about your path. This alignment helps you understand where you want to go and which steps are necessary to get there.

2. **Inner Strength and Confidence:**

   ° An authentic decision strengthens your self-trust. You believe in your abilities and judgment, reinforcing your resolve for future decisions.

3. **Freedom from Doubt:**

   ° When your choices stem from your core essence, doubt and uncertainty diminish. You stand firm in your decision because you know it reflects your truth.

4. **More Energy and Focus:**

   ° A clear decision frees up energy previously trapped in inner conflict. With renewed focus, you can pursue your goals with greater commitment and determination.

5. Growth and Fulfillment:

- By making decisions that resonate with your authentic self, you enable personal growth and experience a deep sense of fulfillment. You live a life that truly reflects who you are.

6. Positive Impact on Relationships:

- Your clarity and self-assurance attract authentic and supportive relationships. People who respect and appreciate your true nature will be drawn to your confidence.

7. A Life of Integrity:

- A true decision leads to a life in harmony with your highest values. You act in accordance with your beliefs, fostering a life of integrity and respect.

By making true decisions, you open the door to a life that is not only successful but also fulfilling and authentic. You shape your reality as an expression of your true self, bringing you deep satisfaction and inner peace. If YOU turn the page NOW, you have made YOUR DECISION!

The Shift

And now, the shift begins! It's time to stop dwelling on what went wrong, who hurt you, or whether something is wrong with you. Enough. Stop wasting your energy on these shadow creations—never again. Bless it all and start living your life as the radiant, magnificent soul that you truly are. Stop tearing yourself down. You are brilliant. You are breathtaking.

Make the shift today—because if you don't, you'll keep holding onto all the negativity, voluntarily keeping yourself trapped in a cycle of suffering. By staying in these low energies, you only attract more of them. Remember: whoever digs in the mud will only find more mud. **No**. If you are ready to let go of these last negative thoughts about yourself, then you are free! And let me tell you this: Enjoy your life! No matter your height, your clothing size, where you live, or what you do—never limit yourself again. The moment you step into your true energetic essence, everything in your life transforms.

Rise—rise into your magical energy! Step into all the beauty, love, and power that is already available to you.

Now, take a moment and imagine this: YOU hold a golden key in your hand—the key to a life filled with joy, passion, and ease. A life where you are constantly uplifted, inspired, and in love with your existence. And the only way to step into it is by releasing the shadows of the past.

Enough. No more losing yourself in the past—no more replaying what happened, who hurt you, or the false belief that something is wrong with you. Those stories are in your past, and it's time to stop giving them power over your life today. You don't have to waste another moment belittling yourself or dwelling on old wounds.

Instead, bless everything with golden love—the experiences, the people, the lessons. See them as sacred parts of your journey, thank them, and then release them with peace. In doing so, you create space for a future overflowing with miracles and infinite possibilities.

Allow yourself to be the radiant, unstoppable soul you were always meant to be. Turn your focus to your brilliance and recognize the breathtaking power that has been inside you all along. You are extraordinary. You are divine. Every part of you is worth celebrating. Today is the day—make the decision. Leave the old shadows behind and step boldly into your true power. The moment you release the past, your spirit soars, and you ascend into your highest, most luminous energy. Here, in this magnetic force of light, lies your ability to turn your life into a masterpiece.

This is your exquisite journey of freedom and rebirth. Let your inner light shine unapologetically, and create the extraordinary life that has been waiting for you all along.

An Empowering Declaration of Your Strength

Date:

"Today, I make a powerful decision—one that liberates my heart and elevates my spirit. I choose to never again believe in the shadow creations that once tried to dim my light. The time has come to say goodbye to old patterns of darkness and leave these illusions behind for good.

Never again will I descend into the realms of fear, pain, abuse, or panic. I choose to release anger and everything that once tried to hold me small. These emotions no longer belong to my story.

Today, I reaffirm my choice to live in the light—a life filled with love, trust, and joy. I open myself to the limitless possibilities that lie ahead, knowing with certainty that my inner light guides and protects me.

I dedicate my energy to healing, growth, and the creation of positivity. Every experience becomes an opportunity to shape my life with intention and awareness. With each breath, I feel the freedom that comes with this decision, and I sense my true self blossoming. From this moment forward, I declare this chapter of shadows **closed**. I step forward with my head held high, carried by the gentle breeze of a new beginning. I am ready to embrace the strength and magic of my being, walking my unique path with confidence and ease. Starting today, I choose the magnificent levels of consciousness that are available to me!"

DONE!
May this declaration strengthen your resolve and guide you toward a life filled with light.
CELEBRATE YOURSELF!

Connection with Earth and the Universe

To enhance grounding and establish a deep connection with both Earth and the Universe, specific exercises and practices can help develop a balanced foot chakra and strengthen your bond with your Higher Self. Here are some suggestions:

Grounding Exercises:

1. Walking Barefoot:

  ○ **Practice:** Spend a few minutes each day walking barefoot on natural surfaces such as grass, sand, or soil. This fosters a sense of grounding and connection with Mother Earth.
  Mindfulness meditation or visualizations where a huge, golden beam of light shoots out of your feet into Mother Earth. Anchoring yourself there and then returning to you 100 times, given as a gift by Mother Earth, can help to strengthen the connection to the earth.

2. Tree Visualization:

  ○ **Practice:** Imagine yourself as a tree. Golden roots extend from the soles of your feet deep into the Earth, providing stability and absorbing nourishing energy. Above, you are a magnificent tree with a vast, radiant canopy! This exercise strengthens your sense of grounding and connection with nature.

3. Gardening:

  ○ **Practice:** Spend time in the garden, plant flowers or vegetables, and feel the soil with your hands. This physical activity naturally enhances grounding and deepens your bond with the Earth.

Connection to the Universe:

1. Stargazing:

- ○ **Practice:** Take time to observe the night sky and feel the vastness of the universe. This practice opens your awareness to your connection with the cosmos. As you do this, visualize a giant golden beam of light shooting from your head, anchoring itself in the universe, in the Divine, and returning to you a hundred times stronger, completely filling you with its energy.

2. Cosmic Breathing:

- ○ **Practice:** Breathe deeply and imagine that each inhale is a golden breath. Golden energy from the universe fills you, and as you exhale, you release this golden positivity back into the world. This strengthens the connection between you and the universe.

3. Affirmations:

- ○ **Practice:** Use affirmations like "I am connected to the universe" or "I receive universal wisdom." Repeat them regularly to deepen your awareness of your universal connection.

The Golden Meditation for Connecting with Earth and the Universe:

Golden Light Beam Meditation

1. Find a Comfortable Seat:

- Sit in a relaxed position, ensuring that your feet touch the ground. Close your eyes and take a few deep breaths to calm your mind.

2. Grounding with Mother Earth:

- Visualize a golden beam of light flowing down from the soles of your feet into the earth, reaching deep into its crystalline core. This light anchors itself firmly and then returns to you, amplified, nourishing you with Mother Earth's energy. Feel the stability and strength flowing back into your energy field and your body. Enjoy how the golden light transforms everything within and around you that is not in alignment with light, love, and joy.

3. Connecting with the Universe:

- Now, imagine another golden beam of light emerging from the crown of your head, ascending into the sky and into the vast universe. It anchors itself in the Divine and returns to you, magnified. Let this golden energy uplift your spirit and strengthen your connection with the vastness of the universe. Feel how it effortlessly spreads throughout your energy field and body! Enjoy it and notice how the gold takes everything in you and around you away that is not light, love and joy!

4. Sense the Connection:

- ○ Enjoy both connections simultaneously and feel the energy of Mother Earth flowing into you while universal energy fills you from above. You are a bridge between heaven and earth—balanced, aligned, and deeply connected. Simply receive this energy; it is your birthright!

5. Remain in This State:

- ○ Stay in this harmonious connection for a few minutes and allow yourself to bask in the balance and tranquility. Feel how the golden energy works within and around you—balancing, transforming, recoding, regenerating, sorting, and healing as needed. You can also consciously direct this golden energy towards any specific fears or areas in your body that need healing. There are no limits to what you can achieve with this light!

6. Returning tot he Present:

- ○ When you are ready, slowly bring awareness back to your body by making small movements. Open your eyes and take in your surroundings, knowing that the golden connections remain intact.

By regularly practicing this meditation, which you can also find on my YouTube Channel, you can strengthen and balance your grounding with the Earth and your connection to the Universe. If you need further guidance or support, I am happy to assist you!

I Bring Luck

On the creative level, there is only abundance and wealth in everything. There is no lack, no fear, no rush, haste, or urgency as found in the energy of competition.

Once you leave this deep level, you will quickly realize that absolutely no one can take anything away from you, nor do you need to act frantically, because there is enough for everyone—and you are CARED FOR!

If you think someone has taken your dream job away from you, trust that something much better will soon appear for you. Something even greater and more wonderful will reveal itself!

As I said, on the creative level, there is no shortage of anything—so be creative, don't let yourself be discouraged, and create!

The creative level is the energetic substance that is simply waiting for you to use it. You are the most wonderful and abundant being, and you can create the most wonderful and abundant things that exist.

From my perspective, the moment someone falls into hurry, haste, fear, or competition, they step out of this powerful creative energy and into shadow creations.

Once you fully leave the energy of competition and scarcity, gratitude will unfold within you. Gratitude—the most beautiful energy in the universe!

I mention gratitude in every aspect of my work and books because I personally always want to be surrounded by the energy of gratitude—because it is golden.

(I even wrote the book *My Book of Gratitude* to help you focus on gratitude, love, joy, and golden energy—every single day.)

This, in turn, connects you with your higher levels and, of course, with trust. Trust in divine protection, divine justice, divine love, divine wisdom, and divine abundance!

I decided as a child to live in trust and in a mindset of abundance and multiplication—NONSTOP—because the universe has shown it to me. The universe reflects it on all levels, and that's exactly what I want to experience in all areas of my life. I can say this from personal experience—not only have I seen it, but the universe has proven these laws and consciousness levels to me. Receiving what you need out of nothing. I KNOW I can trust the universe. Completely! Making the invisible visible is the most magical thing there is.

I have an unshakable belief within me that I always exist in the substance of expansion and goodness and that this energy inspires, fulfills, and permeates me—into every molecule of my being and every cell of my body.

Everything I do, I do with the firm conviction that I am a person who is constantly evolving and, in doing so, brings happiness to EVERYONE and creates incredible progress!

I bring luck and take others with me!

Say it to yourself:

"I bring luck and take others with me!"

Adopt this mindset forever—say to yourself in short form:

"I bring luck!"

The universe rejoices in this and can bring you even more luck!

I always say to myself, **"EVERYONE grows by my side!"**

Isn't that beautiful? Adopt it for yourself, internalize it, let it sink into your subconscious, and let your inner team always cheer you on!

I know it. I feel it. I see it! I am rich, and in this belief of abundance, in this substance of wealth, in this frequency of prosperity, I make everyone rich! There is enough for EVERYONE, because we are all souls, we are all energy, and therefore, there are no boundaries between you and me!

I am rich, and so are all the people around me! I share my knowledge from my abundance, allowing others to benefit from me and grow alongside me. There is only abundance—in me and in others.

When you internalize this, you leave the realm of shadows and step into what you truly are: a unique, creative being.

You must understand that this worldly lack was deliberately placed and is a shadow energy—because this is how people become controllable.

But when you recognize your soul again—your substance, power, abundance, and all the higher levels of consciousness—you are free!

Then you are a magical, free, and happy being! I know this!

It hurts my heart when people get caught up in shadow energy and begin to believe that this dense energy, with all its aspects, is their true nature.

I give my all every day so that people can step into their own power and bring their potential into the world!

Always make sure that you give more value to others than the financial value you receive from them.

And remember: Everything you give returns to you tenfold—or even a million times over!

On the frequency of creation, there is only GROWTH.

Growth is creation—it is the knowing that there is only abundance, power, infinite love, health, wealth, beauty, joy, success, ideas, and soul!

There will only be peace when people reconnect with their unique creative power and use it—because then they will know they are souls! Unfortunately, unrest, conflict, and inner and outer wars will continue as long as shadow creations exist—with all their abuses of power, competition, heaviness, and anger…

As long as this continues, couples who once loved each other will fight over possessions, children, money, and honor—even battling to prove who stands above the other and who "wins."

Instead of recognizing that everything is growth, that we have grown in different directions, that we have outgrown each other, but we can treat each other with respect and, for example, show the children that it is not about destroying the other person or "winning" against them, it is simply about using the creative power and finding and achieving a new level.

Letting Go of the Shadows in Our Lives and Reconnecting with Our Inner Light

Here are some suggestions:

1. Mindfulness and Meditation:

- **Daily Practice:** Start your day with a short mindfulness or meditation exercise. Sit in a quiet place, close your eyes, and focus on your breath. Let go of all thoughts and fears, directing your attention only to the present moment and the golden light surrounding you.
- **Light Visualization:** Imagine how, with every breath, a warm, golden light flows into your body. Allow this light to dissolve all shadows within you until you feel completely nourished and strengthened.

2. Practicing Gratitude:

- **Daily Gratitude Journal:** Write down things you are grateful for every day. This shifts your focus from lack and fear to abundance and positivity. (Feel free to use my book "My Book of Gratitude")

3. Affirmations:

- **Positive Self-Affirmation:** Use affirmations—you can find them at the end of this book, or in my books *"I Am the Love of My Life"* or *"Mindset of a Winner."* Repeat your chosen affirmations daily to align your subconscious with positive thoughts and energies.

4. Grounding:

- **Connection with Nature:** Spend time in nature to automatically regenerate your torus field and gain stability and clarity.

5. Letting Go Through Writing:

- **Free Writing:** Use writing as a tool to release all your fears and shadows onto paper. Without overthinking, write down everything that weighs on you. Then, symbolically burn this paper (safely!) to strengthen the process of letting go and create space for all the positive things in your life.

6. Loving Inner-Child Meditation:

- **Inner Embrace:** Visualize yourself as a child and embrace yourself inwardly with love and acceptance. Recognize that it is safe to feel fear and that you are now capable of caring for this inner child. Take it with you into your present, showing it: "You never have to go back. From today on, you are safe with me—I protect you." Your inner child rests peacefully in your heart.

7. Conscious Breathing:

- **Deep Breathing:** When fear or negative thoughts arise, concentrate on taking deep, but quick breaths. Breathe in deeply but quickly twice and then breathe out. Immediately after that, breathe in twice again, stomach and chest, then breathe out again and let go of everything that you have held in your body. This frees your nervous system and then calms it down! You will immediately notice how it clears your mind.

These practices can help you release inner shadows and reconnect with your own soul, with ease and joy.

Changing Your Mindset

Be ready to step forward—decide today to change your mindset and be proud of the path you've already taken. Now, you will fully embrace and use your creative power!
I am honestly proud and deeply grateful for who I am, for what I have made out of my experiences, and for what I do—I radiate it into this magical world. And I hope YOU do the same. Be proud of yourself, be grateful, and shine your soul's essence into this world—unmistakably, because it is as unique as your personal fingerprint.
With the new mindset you are creating right now, you will become a magnet for goodness, for light, love, joy, abundance, and expansion.
People are naturally drawn to places and individuals that offer growth, strength, success, happiness, and progress on all levels.
I am truly a person, a soul, that desires expansion and happiness for everyone, because, as I said, I know this is what the Universe intends.
Be the best version of yourself, live it, show it, be it!
You will be amazed at how quickly you evolve and incredibly surprised by the success you achieve in all areas of your life.
"What I want for myself, I want for others too!"—for me, that is true love.

1. Shifting from Scarcity Thinking to Abundance Thinking:

- **Believe in abundance:** Instead of focusing on what is missing, shift your focus to what you already have and what is still possible. Trust that there is enough for everyone and that you too can experience prosperity and success.

2. Transforming Self-Doubt into Self-Confidence:

- **Strengthen your self-worth:** Acknowledge your abilities and talents. Remind yourself of past successes and use them as proof of your potential. Celebrate every step you take upward! Every step into higher levels of awareness is a success—celebrate your wins!

3. Turning Negative Thoughts into Positive Ones:

- **Positive reframing:** Whenever you catch yourself thinking negatively, pause and consider how you can reframe the thought into something more positive and constructive. Or immediately start repeating positive affirmations.

4. Shifting from a Victim Mentality to Taking Responsibility:

- **Take ownership:** Recognize that you have the power to create change in your life. Let go of the victim role and embrace your ability to proactively tackle challenges— because you are a soul!

5. Letting Go of Perfectionism:

- **Embrace imperfection:** Understand that perfection is not necessary and that mistakes are opportunities to learn. Allow yourself to be imperfect and still move forward. It's okay if things don't work out perfectly right away.

6. Cultivating Collaboration Instead of Competition:

- **Encourage cooperation:** See others not as competitors, but as partners in both personal and professional areas. A strong network can achieve far more than a lone fighter.

7. From a Rigid Mindset to a Growth Mindset:

- **Learn and evolve:** Welcome challenges as opportunities to learn. Trust that you can grow through perseverance and that you have long ago provided yourself with the right tools for each challenge.

8. Cultivating Gratitude Instead of Dissatisfaction:

- **Practice gratitude:** Keep a gratitude journal and regularly write down things you are grateful for. This increases happiness and helps you maintain a positive mindset.

9. Transforming Fear into Courage:

- **Choose courage over fear:** Understand that courage is not the absence of fear, but the decision to act despite it. Consciously step out of your comfort zone in order to grow.

No More Deals

Stop making deals with fear, panic, and the shadow realm. You don't need that anymore. You have uncovered this illusion, and now you know who and what you truly are—you understand what is available to you in your true light realms, levels of consciousness, and soul dimensions.

No more deals!

Let me explain what I mean.

You know that your energy always flows in the direction of your focus. Wherever your energy goes, your emotions follow. Where your energy goes, your emotions go, your thoughts are created from this, and of course actions arise from this! Actions are real, tangible expressions in this world—they are what you manifest into reality. It doesn't just stay in an energetic field; it materializes.

Remember the Torus field.

Your actions are decisions pulled into your lived, thought, and felt energy here on Earth. So, now we know that every decision, every action triggers a flow of energy and naturally a reaction from people, from the world, from the energy fields, from the universe. Everything in this world lives from action and reaction or vice versa, a reaction, an action.

Take a moment to consider what happens when every one of your actions is triggered by the energy of fear, panic, or a shadow creation?

What kind of reactions do you think you will receive? And even more importantly, what happens when your fear- and panic-driven actions meet an even greater fear- and panic-filled reaction?

I think we don't need to paint that picture here!

But what happens when your focus, your wonderful energy, your actions, and your decisions are fully directed toward the positive?

A firework of goodness will come back to you and fill your entire life.

Never forget that stress and a prolonged survival mode can significantly burden the brain and mental well-being. To counteract this and promote healing, there are specific exercises and practices that can help reduce stress levels and strengthen the health of both mind and body.
Here are some effective methods summarized:

1. Breathwork:

- **Deep Breathing:** Lie down comfortably and place one hand on your belly and the other on your chest. Inhale deeply through your nose twice—first filling your belly, then your chest—and exhale quickly through your mouth. In, in, out. In, in, out. This type of breathing activates the parasympathetic nervous system, promoting relaxation by releasing anything stuck within your body. Your breath will flow through all levels of your consciousness, opening everything up so that you can once again become the magical, golden vessel through which your soul can shine.

2. Progressive Muscle Relaxation:

- **Tense and Release:** Consciously work through different muscle groups in your body by tensing them and then letting go, naturally synchronized with your breathing. This practice helps release physical tension and creates a deep sense of relaxation.

3. Mindfulness Meditation:

- **Presence in the Moment:** Sit in a quiet place, focus on your breath, and observe each thought without judgment before gently bringing your attention back to your breath. Ask Archangel Metatron to support you and deepen your mindfulness. This practice helps you embrace gentleness, let go, and cultivate inner peace. It promotes a calm mind, reduces stress symptoms, and lowers the release of stress hormones.

4. Physical Movement:

*   **Regular Activity:** Find a form of physical exercise that brings you joy, whether it's walking, running, yoga, tennis, or dancing. Movement releases endorphins, which help reduce stress and strengthen the brain.

5. Improve Sleep Hygiene:

*   **Consistent Sleep Schedule:** Maintain a healthy sleep cycle by going to bed and waking up at the same time each day. Restorative sleep is essential for the brain's healing and recovery. Before sleeping, call upon Archangel Raphael and ask him to surround you, so you can rest peacefully and feel protected.

6. Nutrition and Hydration:

*   **Balanced Diet:** Ensure your diet is rich and well-balanced, incorporating antioxidants, minerals, and vitamins to support brain health. Don't forget to drink enough water. On my website, you'll find two amazing products that I collaborate with.

7. Mental Exercises:

*   **Brain Training:** Engage in puzzles, crosswords, or other thinking games that stimulate the brain and enhance its function. These exercises help maintain and improve cognitive abilities.

8. Strengthening Social Bonds:

- **Positive Interactions:** Social support is essential for mental health. Spend time with family and friends who uplift you and help foster positive emotions while reducing stress. You can easily call upon Lakshmi in your life—she brings connection!

9. Visualization and Goal Setting:

- **Creating Positive Images:** Regularly visualize positive scenarios or goals, just as you learned in the layout level! This "golden canvas" technique helps train your brain to focus on positive outcomes and reduce stress.

By integrating these practices into your daily life, you can effectively lower stress levels and align both your mind and mindset toward healing and positive transformation. Be patient with yourself and recognize that healing takes time and consistent care.
Never fear your own light—embrace it! Rejoice in your light, your soul, your beauty, and your limitless potential.

Welcome to the Magical World of Energies

Let me take you on a wondrous journey deep into the mystery and magic of the unseen realms. It is a world that exists beyond physical reality—a world that comes to life through my clairvoyance, offering you glimpses into the astral plane, the universe, the magical helpers, the souls, and the energies that surround us.

The Astral World: A Dimension of Magic

In the astral world, a universe unfolds, radiating with light and vitality. This realm, unrestricted by physical laws, pulses in a kaleidoscope of colors, frequencies, and vibrations. Here, souls dance in shapes and patterns beyond the grasp of the human eye, yet they are of infinite beauty.

This world is filled with the unconditional love and wisdom of astral guides—beings of light who are always ready to support and guide us. Their presence is a constant reminder that we are never alone, that help is always near, if only we choose to open ourselves to it.

The Energies That Surround Us

On Earth, in our everyday existence, we are surrounded by an invisible web of energies—our aura. These energies flow within and around us, carrying stories of joy, hope, and even challenges. Through my clairvoyance, I perceive the aura and energy fields surrounding every living being—vibrant reflections of our inner worlds.

Every movement, thought, and emotion leaves an imprint, influencing the energetic balance of the entire planet. By becoming aware of these energies, we recognize the unbreakable connection between all of us.

The Origin of Souls: A Cosmic Wonder

Every soul emerges from the divine source—a luminous wellspring of light and love. This primordial energy is our true home, a familiar melody resonating deep within us, connecting us to our higher self, our divine essence. The soul's journey is a return to this indescribable beauty and wholeness.

Through encounters with our own soul, new dimensions of understanding and acceptance unfold. It is an invitation to embrace our essence with open arms and step fully into our true purpose.

The Magical Power of Love

Everything we experience in these realms is held together by the magic of love. It is the driving force behind every atomic dance, every striving for growth, and every act of connection. In love, we find the answers to our deepest questions and the healing for all our wounds. Let this be an invitation to explore your own soul and discover the beauty that awaits you in every moment of your life. May this journey inspire you to embrace the magic of the energetic realms with courage and joy. Love yourself, for you are worthy of love. You are love—inside and out. Live your magical power of love for yourself and then share it with the world.

I hope these words bring this wondrous world into your heart and home.

See it with your third eye, feel it with your heart, let your Higher Mind whisper it to you, and allow your soul to illuminate you with its wisdom!

Cord Cutting

Cord Cutting is a powerful energetic practice that helps dissolve unwanted or burdensome energetic connections of all kinds. These connections, often referred to as "energy cords" or "ties," can form over time with people, places, or situations that influence us in various ways. Such energetic bonds may drain our energy and prevent us from fully living in our own power and clarity.

Meaning of Cord Cuttings:

1. **Energetic Freedom**: Cord Cutting allows us to release energetic burdens and free ourselves from influences that no longer serve us.
2. **Emotional Clarity**: By severing these connections, emotional ties linked to pain, fear, or trauma can be healed.
3. **Strengthening the Self**: It enables you to reclaim your own energy and step into your own power.
4. **Encouraging Growth**: Without the weight of old energies, you can grow freely and welcome new experiences without hesitation or limitation.

Just like clearing a garden of weeds, Cord Cutting consciously dissolves energetic ties that no longer contribute to our highest good. It is an act of self-care that regularly helps us create space in which we can flourish. Freed from heavy, grounding energies, we gain clarity, vitality, and the freedom to shape our lives with intention. Cord Cutting brings light into the areas that often burden us unconsciously, giving us the opportunity to release attachments and emotions that no longer serve us. It is about letting go of the energetic threads that deplete our energy reserves and hinder our full potential.

Without the distraction of old connections, you can focus your energy on what truly matters and brings you joy. Cord Cutting is not just an act of releasing but also a powerful step toward a more conscious and fulfilling life. By regularly reviewing and clearing old connections, you maintain your energetic space and shape the energy pattern of your life in harmony and light.

Cord Cutting Exercise with the Help of Archangel Michael, Ganesh, Kali and Maat:

Now, let's learn how to sever these energetic ties. Enjoy the process!

Preparation:
1. **Find a Quiet Place:** Sit comfortably, relax your body, and take a few deep breaths in and out. Center yourself and feel the nourishing golden light flowing from Mother Earth and the Universe. You are completely enveloped in this energy.
2. **Set a Clear Intention:** State in your mind or aloud that you wish to dissolve all energetic connections that do not align with light, love, and joy and that hinder you from being your true self.

The Practice:
1. **Call Upon Archangel Michael:** Ask Archangel Michael to use his mighty sword of light to sever all energetic ties that no longer serve your highest good—regardless of time, dimension, situation, karma, or whether these connections are small silken threads, thick cords, rubber bands, chains, entanglements, or sticky attachments. It doesn't matter whether these ties go from you to someone else or from someone else to you. Visualize him gently yet decisively cutting these ties as you breathe deeply, feeling all remaining fragments being removed.
2. **Ask Ganesh:** Invite Ganesh to remove all obstacles that may be preventing you from fully letting go. Imagine his energy

clearing all blockages and cleansing every negative connection completely.

3. **Summon Kali:** Picture Kali with her fearless and transformative energy, setting all negative energies and connections ablaze, purifying and transmuting them into light.

4. **Ask Maat for Balance:** Invoke Maat to help restore balance and healing after the Cord Cutting process. Visualize her feather of truth, clarity, and love bringing harmony to your heart and soul.

Closing:

- **Express Gratitude:** Thank Archangel Michael, Ganesh, Kali, and Maat for their support and guidance, as well as your own golden energy.
- **Grounding and Reconnection:** Imagine a golden light beam flowing from your feet deep into the Earth, grounding you. At the same time, a golden laser beam from your crown chakra extends into the Universe, drawing back a hundredfold stronger golden energy, filling you completely. Feel how radiant you are now!
- **Return to the Present Moment:** Take a deep breath, move your body slightly, and open your eyes, fully present in the here and now.

This practice can help you free yourself from old, non-serving energies and rediscover your personal power. Perform it as often as it feels right for you to enhance clarity and freedom in your energy and soul life.

Releasing Foreign Energies

Foreign energies are energetic influences that do not belong to your natural energy system but can still affect you. These energies can originate from various sources and take different forms:

Origins of Foreign Energies:
1. **Emotional Energy from Others**: Sometimes, we absorb the emotions and moods of others, especially when we are near them or have an emotional connection. This can happen consciously or unconsciously.
2. **Negative Environments:** Places with high levels of stress, conflict, or sadness can retain such energies in their atmosphere, which we may take on.
3. **Unresolved Conflicts:** Emotional or energetic ties to people from the past, especially when unresolved matters exist, can act as foreign energies.
4. **Energetic "Residues":** When interacting with others or different situations, energetic "residues" from shadow creations can linger or be absorbed, especially if you are empathic or highly sensitive.

Effects of Foreign Energies:
- **Emotional Confusion:** You may experience feelings or thoughts that are uncharacteristic of you, leading to confusion or discomfort.
- **Energy Drain:** Carrying foreign energies can be exhausting, as they can deplete your own energy.
- **Impaired Decision-Making:** Foreign energies can cloud your clarity and ability to make decisions by overshadowing your true thoughts and emotions.

Managing Foreign Energies:

To minimize the impact of foreign energies, it is essential to engage in regular energetic cleansing practices, such as the following meditation, the previously learned Cord Cutting, and, of course, working with golden energies! Additionally, setting clear emotional and energetic boundaries helps reduce the absorption of foreign energies—especially when consciously distancing yourself from shadow creations.

By cultivating awareness of your own energy, you will develop discernment between what truly belongs to you and what does not—between the illusions of the shadow plane and the divine source. Trust me, this will quickly become evident, bringing you into a healthier and more balanced energetic state.

Now, I will show you how to release foreign energies and reclaim your own true energy with the support of Archangel Michael, Archangel Raphael, and the Divine Mother:

Exercise: Returning to Your True Energy

Preparation:
1. **Find a quiet space:** Sit comfortably, close your eyes, and take a few deep, calming breaths to center yourself. Find your inner balance and feel the nourishing golden light flowing from Mother Earth and the Universe, wrapping around you completely.
2. **Set your intention:** Declare in your mind or out loud that you are ready to release all foreign energies and fully restore your own energy.

The Exercise:
1. **Call upon Archangel Michael:** Ask Archangel Michael to surround you with his protective blue and golden light. Imagine this light gently dissolving and removing all foreign energies from your energy field. Say: *"Beloved Archangel Michael, I have now chosen to release all foreign energies. At this moment, all foreign energies leave my entire energy field and return to where they belong and originated—now, for the highest good of all!"* Visualize and feel how he guides these energies back to their original sources.

2. **Invite Archangel Raphael:** Call upon Archangel Raphael to flood your energy field with his golden and emerald-green healing light. This divine light will help seal any gaps and restore your true energy. Say: *"Dear Archangel Raphael, I ask you to bring back all of my true energy with your golden light— all the energy I may have given away, that was taken from me, or that I lost somewhere. Let all my energy now return to me, settling in the perfect place within my entire energy*

83

system. Thank you! Please strengthen my energy field now, so that I may be harmonious and whole."

3. **Connect with the Divine Mother**: Ask the Divine Mother to wrap you in her infinite love and protection. Like a warm embrace, her energy surrounds and shields you. Visualize how she calls back any remaining lost energy into your being, regenerating and replenishing your essence. Feel deep gratitude for her love.

Integration:
- **Visualization:** See and feel your own true energy flowing back into you in a gentle stream of golden light, filling your cells and your entire being until you are completely yourself again.
- **Gratitude:** Express your thanks to Archangel Michael, Archangel Raphael, and the Divine Mother for their assistance and protection throughout this process.

Returning:
1. **Grounding and Connecting with Your Higher Consciousness:** Imagine your golden connection to the Earth deepening as roots grow from your feet, grounding you firmly into the earth. At the same time, visualize your light beam shooting up from your head into the universe, traveling through your levels of consciousness, reaching your higher heart and your oversoul.
2. **Conscious Breathing:** Take a few deep breaths, open yourself to universal love, then gently open your eyes. Move slightly to bring your awareness fully back to the present moment.

This practice will help you lovingly release foreign energies and anchor your own pure energy within yourself. By practicing regularly, you will experience a deeper sense of clarity and connection with your true self in daily life.

The Golden Canvas – For Releasing

The Golden Canvas is a powerful tool for transformation, helping us turn the negative aspects of our lives into light and peace. It offers a safe space to release everything that burdens us and keeps us in the shadows, allowing these energies to dissolve into positive and healing vibrations.

How to Use the Golden Canvas:

1. Prepare Yourself:

- Find a quiet place where you won't be disturbed. Sit comfortably, close your eyes, and take deep breaths in and out to center yourself and calm your mind. Connect with your inner balance and feel the nourishing golden light flowing from Mother Earth and the Universe. You are completely wrapped in this radiant energy.

2. Visualize the Golden Canvas:

- In your mind's eye, imagine a large, shimmering canvas made of pure gold, nourished by both Mother Earth and the Universe. This canvas is alive, flowing, and filled with pure golden energy, ready to receive and transform all the energies you wish to release.

3. Transfer the Shadows:

- Mentally place all negative experiences onto the canvas— your fears, worries, painful situations, and even people who challenge you. Feel how these energies gently detach from your body and mind and are released onto the Golden Canvas.

4. Begin the Transformation:

- Watch as the gold of the canvas lovingly absorbs, embraces, and transforms every burden into light and wisdom. The canvas tirelessly works to turn all darkness into radiant brilliance.

5. Receive the Golden Dust:

- Imagine that as this transformation takes place, a fine golden dust emerges and softly falls upon you. This golden dust is filled with healing, peace, and renewed energy. Feel how it cleanses and strengthens you, penetrating every cell of your body and filling every molecule of your aura with divine light.

6. Hand Over the Canvas:

- Now, in your mind, hand over the Golden Canvas—filled with the transformed energies—to the Divine Mother and Christ. See how they lovingly receive it and lift it into the universe, where it merges into the golden light, further amplifying healing and peace. As this happens, the golden dust continues to rain down upon you, blessing you with divine love and renewal.

7. Express Gratitude:

- Give thanks to the Divine Mother and Christ for their presence and support. Feel deep gratitude in your heart for the transformation you have experienced.

8. Return:

- Bring your awareness back to the room, gently open your eyes, and take a moment to enjoy the peace and light now flowing through you.

This simple yet powerful practice allows you to truly let go of past burdens, transforming them into a source of inner strength, blessings, and positivity. By regularly working with the Golden Canvas, you will recognize your own ability to turn every challenge into an opportunity for healing, growth, and divine transformation.

The Golden Canvas- Learn to Manifest

When I sit down and think about my desires, I let my imagination and fantasy run completely free. As children, most of us did this naturally—it is our true power.
People used to tell me that I was living in a dream world.
Do you know this feeling? Have you experienced the same?
Diving into imagination and fantasy was often portrayed as something bad! But in truth, it is the greatest power we possess. And yes, it *is* the dream world! The dream world of the layout level, which allows us to dream freely.
As a child, you probably, like me, automatically immersed yourself in your imagination to unfold the creative power that we all possess!
This creative force allows us to create everything; it is the magical substance of creation that is available to us in the universe.
We use this creative force through our mind because the soul knows exactly what it wants to express through our body.
Your mental power, imagination, and creative force are the bridge between your soul and your body, between the invisible and the visible!
Use your imagination and express the magic of your soul through your body. This is our task, our beauty—to unfold all the abundance and love here on Earth.
See yourself as a whole, not just as one part. You are all levels of consciousness united in one! Never make the mistake of focusing on only one aspect—such as only your body while neglecting the great creative power of your mind or your soul. Or focusing only on spiritual growth but forgetting how to truly live!
Use everything in harmony. Now you can—because you are aware of it.
You are the most WONDERFUL and ABUNDANT BEING there is.
Thankfully, no one could ever divert me from my path because I can truly *see* this so-called fantasy world! I see the energies, the endless dance of creation. My angels have been with me all my life, and I have continuously developed my gift, creating concepts that *anyone* can apply.

Everyone has imagination and can use it—because everyone has a third eye! Imagination is directly linked to the third eye. Everyone has it and can use it. Maybe yours needs to be reactivated, cleansed of all the terrible shadows. That may be the case—but that is exactly what you are doing right now.

To me, the third eye is the expression of the soul. So, when you use your imagination and creative power, you are closest to your soul. On the soul level, everything happens through this frequency of creation. There are no limits—unless we create them ourselves!

If you can see your goal, then it already exists for you. Everything is already present in infinite abundance. You don't need to destroy anything or take anything from anyone else—that is impossible, because the substance is already there.

As soon as you hold a vision and do not let it go, the universe is obligated to create it—through you!

If you know what you want, write it down. Write it down and describe to yourself what you see.

Bring your vision to your Golden Canvas as often as you can, and tell yourself: "I don't know how, but I know this is the truth!" It doesn't matter if others believe in you—the most important thing is that you believe in yourself, that you feel, smell, taste, and experience it!

I constantly challenge myself with things beyond my current reach. Dare to dream big and never give up! That is the only difference between successful and unsuccessful people. A successful person never gives up.

But avoid energies of envy, self-doubt, or letting people laugh at your dreams. Never let these energies enter your imagination and make you insecure.

NEVER!

Work first within yourself, in your soul. Just you and the universe. Align yourself in harmony with your vision, with your dream.

Alignment, balance, peace, harmony, and equilibrium—these are the energies you need to attract your desires and goals.

Your frequency must match the frequency of your dream—then it becomes reality.

You can only attract what you are in harmony with. That's energy—it's all about energetic frequencies and creation.

This automatically moves you away from old frequencies and shifts you into a new vibration. This happens when you use your imagination—your own unique fantasy.

With your imagination—your greatest tool—you can travel into high vibrational frequencies, other dimensions, and even other worlds, reaching the place where everything is created!

I am deeply grateful that I can see all of this and be part of this vast, wonderful universe. It fills me with gratitude and awe to realize how powerful I am—and how powerful YOU are!

Isn't that incredible?

Creation is the most beautiful, magnificent, magical, and incredible force there is. Start using it today. Remember the childlike ease of using your imagination, without limitations or doubts.

When you played as a princess, you became one, fully and completely, with your whole being. When you were a pirate, you were a pirate with your whole heart and soul. Dare to fully embrace your dreams again, to dream big, and to wish for something.

There is nothing wrong with that—quite the opposite! A desire is born from the soul. To me, desires are the way the spiritual world communicates with us, saying: "Please, let me create something wonderful through you!"

Isn't that beautiful?

Desires are the expression of divine substance, which only wants good for us!

Tell yourself:

"I use my creative power now! I can do this, and everything comes to me."

"Every day, I am amazed by the miracles unfolding in my life!"

"Miracle after miracle is happening now!"

"One soul miracle after another unfolds before me!"

Use your imagination and make the invisible visible.

Dreaming kept me alive and gave me a life worth living—even though I probably had the worst possible start one could imagine. Dream and use this wonderful substance of the universe.

Teach your children that they are allowed to dream, to see, to have wishes, and to pursue whatever they want to achieve! Let them listen to their souls and bring forth the gifts they carry within them for this life.

To Manifest, There Are 3 Key Points

Intention: This is what we desire, what we want to express! I listen to myself!

Destiny/Purpose: This is what our soul longs for, what it wants to express through us!

Social Environment- The Energy That Surrounds Us: Is the energy around us truly supporting us or working against us?
We can change it at any time! We can shift, transform, or walk away whenever necessary. Sometimes, this is essential. I left my family because it was destructive. You are allowed to change, to leave, to choose a different path—especially when nothing and no one is truly for you.

Here is a guide on how to use the Golden Canvas to manifest your desires and dreams:

Manifestation with the Golden Canvas

1. Preparation for Manifestation:

- Find a quiet, undisturbed place and sit comfortably. Take deep breaths in and out to center yourself mentally and emotionally. Feel the nourishing golden light beam from Mother Earth and the Universe surrounding you completely.

2. Entering the Layout Level:
- Imagine yourself in a silent, clear sphere of possibilities—the Layout Level. This is the space of pure creation, open and ready to receive your visions. Feel the infinite love surrounding you—you are welcome here.

3. Creating the Golden Canvas:
- Visualize a large, glowing canvas made of golden light before you. It shimmers and radiates, ready to receive your highest intentions, dreams, and visions.

4. Projecting Your Manifestation onto the Canvas:
- Focus on what you wish to manifest: health, love, prosperity, fulfillment—anything you desire. Paint this vision onto the Golden Canvas using vivid images, emotions, and clear thoughts. Be as detailed as possible—either as a picture or a movie. Fill it with emotions—feel the joy and excitement of already having achieved it.

5. Sending the Canvas Through All Levels:

- See the Golden Canvas shining from the Layout Level, passing through all levels of consciousness, reaching every aspect of your being. Feel its energy as it solidifies into reality in your life. The canvas glows brighter and becomes even more alive with your vision.

6. Activating the Power of the Canvas
- Allow the Golden Canvas to send out rays of energy in all directions. These rays attract synchronicities, opportunities, and the right circumstances to bring your dreams into reality.

7. Expressing Gratitude:
- Show gratitude as if your manifestation has already happened. Feel the joy and peace flowing through you from this realization.

8. Integration & Trust:
- Return to the present moment, gently open your eyes, and trust that the Universe has heard your intentions. Know that your desires will manifest in the best possible way.

This powerful manifestation practice helps you stay focused and clear on your goals while inviting the Universe to support the realization of your dreams. Practice regularly to create a fulfilling and authentic life.

Calling Upon Divine Order, Divine Justice and Divine Restoration

Calling upon Divine Order, Divine Justice, and Divine Restoration is a powerful act that helps us bring balance, harmony, and healing into our lives. These are universal principles deeply rooted in many spiritual traditions, guiding us toward inner and outer equilibrium. This energy can be restored through conscious invocation and alignment.

The Meaning of Divine Order, Justice, and Restoration

1. **Divine Order:**

   ○ Divine Order reminds us that there is a higher plan and a coherent structure in the universe. It invites us to trust the natural flow of life and align with its wisdom.

2. **Divine Justice:**

   ○ Divine Justice ensures that true balance and fairness prevail, even if they are not immediately visible. It promises that every being will receive the true harvest of their actions, encouraging forgiveness and letting go of resentment.

3. **Divine Restoration:**

   ○ Divine Restoration represents healing and the reinstatement of love and harmony. It assures us that everything that has fallen out of balance will ultimately find its rightful place. What belongs to you will always return to you!

Activation with Christ & Krishna:

Preparation:
1. **A Moment of Stillness:** Find a quiet place where you can focus and meditate. Center yourself and feel the nourishing golden light from Mother Earth and the Universe surrounding you.
2. **Set Your Intention:** Open your heart to divine presence and ask for guidance and support.

The Practice:

1. **Ask for Support from Christ:**

   ° Imagine Christ standing before you, radiating divine light, ready to support you with his boundless love and wisdom. Ask him to help you restore Divine Order in your life—to find the stillness that reveals the deeper meaning behind everything. Let his light open your heart to understanding and acceptance, and trust that he is bringing everything in your life back into divine harmony.

2. **Call Upon Krishna:**

   ° Visualize Krishna in his many colors and forms, filled with joy and divine wisdom. Ask for his help in experiencing Divine Justice and understanding that everything happening is part of a greater plan and process. Allow his music and playful spirit to fill your heart with peace and balance, and trust that he is restoring divine justice throughout your entire life.

3. Activate Devine Restoration:

- With Christ and Krishna by your side, ask them to initiate the energy of Divine Restoration, healing all imperfections in your life. See how their combined light nurtures every wound, brings hope, and restores harmony. Say to yourself: "*I believe in Divine Restoration. The good that has fallen victim to shadow creations is now being restored and brings only goodness into my life!*"

Integration:
- **Gratitude:** Express your deep gratitude for the support and activation of these divine principles.
- **Returning to Daily Life:** Allow the energies to work within you as you gently return to conscious awareness, integrating the calming power of this experience into your everyday life.

This practice can help you find deep peace and trust by aligning yourself with Divine Order, Justice, and Restoration, guiding you to shape your life with an open heart.
Through a positive state of consciousness, you have the power to transform everything!

Your Golden Timeline

The concept of timelines opens a fascinating perspective on understanding our existence and possibilities. Timelines are conceptual pathways that represent different potential futures, unfolding based on our decisions, thoughts, and actions. Every choice we make strengthens a particular timeline and directs our life in a specific direction.

Timelines: Pathways of Potential

Timelines represent the infinite possibilities that lie ahead. They are the tracks shaped by our conscious and unconscious choices. At any point in our lives, we can turn toward different futures, each offering unique experiences and lessons.

The Soul Line: The Highest Soul Plan

Among these countless timelines, there is a special one known as the golden timeline or soul line. This timeline represents our highest soul plan—the full realization of who we truly are. It is the path of greatest potential and deepest fulfillment, aligning with the core of our spiritual purpose.

The soul line is the path that leads us to our best version—a life filled with love, joy, and authentic expression. It carries the intentions and aspirations we have chosen on a soul level to live a meaningful and fulfilling life.

Activation of the Soul Line with the Higher Self

To live in harmony with your soul line, you can activate this connection through your Higher Self. The Higher Mind is the wise part of your soul that sees the greater perspective and lovingly guides you.

Activation Exercise:

1. **Find a Quiet Place:** Sit down in a peaceful spot, close your eyes, and relax your body. Breathe deeply in and out to clear your mind. Center yourself and feel the nourishing golden light beam from Mother Earth and the Universe. You are fully embraced.

2. **Call Upon Your Higher Mind – Your Higher Self:** Imagine a warm, golden light flowing down from above, completely surrounding you. This light is the essence of your Higher Self, which is always with you.

3. **Connect with Your Soul Line:** Visualize your golden timeline stretching out before you, extending into the future. This line represents the path of your highest soul plan. Step onto it and begin walking. With every step, you manifest your Higher Self and affirm your decision to walk your golden soul path. Feel the energy of this timeline—its clarity, love, and fulfillment.

4. **Set Your Intention:** Ask your Higher Self for guidance in making choices that keep you aligned with this golden timeline. Trust that every decision strengthening this connection will lead you to your highest good.

5. **Receive Wisdom**: Stay in this state of connection and ask your Higher Self for messages or insights that will keep you aligned with your soul line. Trust the answers that come to you.

6. **Return to the Present:** Take a few deep breaths, make small movements, and gently return to the here and now, remembering that you are always connected to your highest path.

By practicing this connection regularly, you strengthen your alignment with your soul line, allowing yourself to experience life in its fullest and most joyful form.

The 12 Soul Levels

You are the most beautiful soul, the most radiant being—words can hardly capture it.
Let's take a look at what Wikipedia says:
Soul = The totality of all emotional impulses and mental processes in a human being.
Is that all?
Of course not.
Let's first consider the three different perspectives:

1- The Spiritual/Religious Perspective

In most spiritual and religious traditions, the soul has been regarded as the immortal, non-material essence within a person. It is often seen as the consciousness of a human being, the core of one's identity, separate from the body.
The soul is closely linked to the subconscious, true self, and capacity for spiritual growth.

2- The Philosophical Perspective

From a philosophical standpoint, the concept of the soul delves into the depth of our being, the essence that grants individuality to a person. Here, the soul is believed to be the seat of emotions, thoughts, and personal experiences. Philosophical discussions often revolve around existence, the connection between body and mind, and the soul's potential immortality.

3- The Metaphorical Perspective:

In this view, the soul is seen as both the deepest aspect of human character and the source of emotions and creativity. It is believed to be the essence that defines a person, including their values, passions, and desires.

You are the soul, in all its facets. Through your soul, you are automatically connected to the universe, the higher power, the oversoul, the intelligent substance, and the collective consciousness. The soul is immortal, indestructible, and capable of traveling through all times, spaces, dimensions, universes, and planes. I wouldn't say this if I didn't know it—I see souls and have the honor of communicating with them when necessary. There is nothing more beautiful than witnessing their pure love, compassion, respect, empathy, understanding, gratitude, grace, joy, and peace.

The blessing of souls showers upon us daily, whether we accept it or not. Every day, we are being blessed. Rediscovering your soul, awakening it, and unfolding its beauty is a lifelong journey—but a magnificent one. On this path, you heal your soul lineage, reintegrate lost soul fragments, and watch your soul's divine plan unfold.

You are your soul. You are a part of the divine whole, the divine substance. Imagine a vast ocean—this is God, the source of everything. The soul is like a dewdrop, separated yet still within the whole. Everything God is, you are as well. That is why it is said that we are created in God's image.

What you accept, you receive.

You get what you tolerate.

It's that simple when it comes to energy. The energy form and level you allow and tolerate is what will manifest in your life. If you settle for shadow levels, they will follow you everywhere. This brings us back to consciousness levels, which exist layered on top of each other. Only when you refuse to tolerate something do you grow beyond it and ascend.

The soul is the most magical light I have ever seen—pure golden light. At its center lies a white core, surrounded by radiant gold, and edged with a soft pink aura.

When we enter the soul plane, we experience 12 levels that surround and protect the soul.

These are the 12 aspects of the soul, safeguarding its essence:

1) Soul Dignity- Worth
2) Soul Joy- Lightness
3) Soul Love- Blessing
4) Soul Growth- Expansion
5) Soul Intuition- Wisdom
6) Soul Grace- Gentleness
7) Soul Humility- Gratitude
8) Soul Peace- Trust
9) Soul Justice- Truth
10) Soul Loyalty- Connection
11) Soul Abundance- Fulfillment
12) Soul Protection- Safety / Courage

All of this is our birthright.
Each and every value listed here is YOUR birthright.
This is who you are; this already exists within you. Everything is present—it only needs to be uncovered, because as energy, it is already there!

SOUL DIGNITY

The level of Soul Dignity is the one directly surrounding the soul. It is the closest to the soul itself. When you feel self-worth, treat yourself and all living beings with value and respect, you strengthen this soul level.
It should be the closest thing to us—self-worth and dignity. Since this is the innermost soul level, you can see that it is your birthright!
I am dignity.
I am the most valuable being that exists.
The Divine Mother and Goddess Dana can help you with this.

Short Prayer:
My dearest Divine Mother and beloved Goddess Dana, please reactivate my God-given Soul Dignity and my inner worth.

I carry them within me, and with every breath, this energy will blossom inside me.
Thank you!

SOUL JOY

This is the second soul level, showing how important joy and lightness truly are. They are the fundamental energies of the universe. If you are spiritually growing, your joy and lightness must grow alongside you. If this is not happening, something is off.
This is always a good indicator of whether you are on the right path!
Joy and lightness are essential.
I am joy.
My being is filled with lightness.
Kuthumi and Lakshmi can assist you with this.

Short Prayer:
My magical Lakshmi and joyful Kuthumi, please make my inner joy and lightness shine brightly.
I know that I am a joyful, vibrant, and laughing being, and I thank you for helping me to live and embody this!
Thank you!

SOUL LOVE

The third level of the soul is the beautiful energy of Soul Love!
Whoever holds love within them, lives it, and shares it is
truly blessed in life.
Love is a blessing.
A heart full of love is the greatest wealth that exists.
The soul is love, the universe is filled with it, and it is the energy from which we are created!
LOVE is EVERYTHING, and EVERYTHING is LOVE.

I am love.
I am loving and lovable.
Mother Mary and Lady Nada can assist you with this.

Short Prayer:
"My most loving and blessed angelic beings, Mother Mary and Lady Nada, please help me fully feel, receive, and share love again.
I am a blessing to this world!
Thank you!"

SOUL DEVELOPMENT

The fourth soul level is the wondrous energy of Soul Development.
The entire universe continuously strives for growth and expansion.
It is a completely natural desire to grow and improve.
There is never a standstill—there is always growth!
Never resist this process—flow with it. Enjoy developing and evolving at any age!
Use the natural power of this soul level to grow into your highest self.
Blossom into one of the most radiant souls, spreading your magic across the world.
I am the substance of eternal growth.
I love to evolve!
Archangel Raziel and Melchizedek can help you wonderfully with this.

Short Prayer:
My beloved Archangel Raziel and wondrous Melchizedek, I lovingly ask you—
bless me with eternal development and growth until my soul is completely liberated
and fully reconnected to the infinite divine love.
I am so grateful for your support!
Thank you!

SOUL INTUITION

Oh, how important our intuition is—our inner feeling, the direct connection to divine guidance that leads us through life.

I love this fifth soul level because it awakens the wisdom within us, reflecting divine knowledge and allowing us to make clear decisions with inner peace.

True wisdom means living in harmony with divine laws, such as:
Vibration – Everything moves.
Constant Transformation – Everything takes form.
Relativity – Everything is relative.
Polarity – Everything has an opposite.
Rhythm – Everything flows in a cycle.
Cause and Effect – Every cause has an effect, and every effect has a cause.
Growth – Everything ripens in its own time.

If you live in alignment with these laws, you can fully access your intuition.
I am deeply connected to divine wisdom.
I embody intuition in my life.
Yogananda and Babaji can assist you in developing this connection.

Short Prayer:
My blessed and beloved Master Yogananda and revered Babaji, I love you deeply and thank you for freeing this fifth level within me. Please help me fully develop my soul's intuition and wisdom. Thank you!

SOUL GRACE

This sixth soul level is truly magical. Imagine if every person had this level fully awakened and lived with divine grace every day!

There would be no more power struggles or competition—only harmony and flow.
So let's awaken this level now and spread humility and gentleness across the Earth!
This level also contains courage within it.
Grace is one of the most beautiful values in the universe—
an expression of dignity and inner beauty.
It gives you the courage to be exactly who you are.
Can you feel the beauty that comes from grace and gentleness and the strength they create?
The moment you embrace them, your energy shifts completely!
Dignity, love, beauty, compassion, empathy, and courage take their rightful place in your heart.
I absolutely love the word Grace!
I am Grace!
As divine grace and gentleness unfold, I strengthen my sixth soul level.
I awaken new courage within me!
Mataji and the Divine Mother can help you with this.

Short Prayer:
I bow before you, Mataji and Divine Mother, in deep reverence for your grace and gentleness.
You bless me with these values, allowing them to blossom in my heart.
Thank you for your sweet love, filling me completely with grace, gentleness, dignity, love, compassion, and empathy.
Thank you!

SOUL HUMILITY

This seventh soul level is often misunderstood. Why?
Because true humility is not about submission or giving up your self-empowerment.

Instead, humility means deep love and gratitude for the creative force of the universe, allowing it to express itself fully through you.

Isn't that beautiful?

This level is filled with humility and gratitude.

As you may already know, I always say that gratitude is the most golden and radiant energy in the universe.

We need gratitude to create and manifest—only through gratitude does divine substance begin to work for us.

I live in deep humility toward the divine creative force.

I am surrounded and filled with golden gratitude.

Christ and Krishna can help you embrace this level.

Short Prayer:

Dearest Christ and Krishna, I am so grateful that you are now by my side. In deep, sincere humility, I bow before you and feel your love and blessing surrounding me.

I use the creative power of the universe for the good of all, for everyone, and for the highest purpose.

Thank you for your divine presence!

SOUL PEACE

The eighth soul level represents inner peace. This peace fills everything—where peace exists, only light, love, joy, and trust remain.

Those who live in peace also possess trust—a divine trust.

In peace and trust, you will always grow—you will never feel lack or struggle again.

Once you activate this beautiful level, peace and trust will flow into all areas of your life.

If all humans had this soul level liberated, we would experience world peace.

We would trust each other again and support one another.

I am peace.
I am peace in my life, in my body, in my work, in my relationships…
I love and live peace and bring trust into the world.
Parvati and Ganesh can assist you in embracing this energy.
This mother-son pair is powerful—Parvati represents peace, while Ganesh embodies trust. How beautiful is that?
Now, allow them both to fill you with their divine presence.

Short Prayer:
Dearest, beautiful Parvati and powerful, delightful Ganesh,
please stand by my side and help me develop inner peace, allowing it to flow into all areas of my life.
From this moment forward, soul peace and deep trust are a permanent part of my being.
I am so grateful for your limitless love and assistance!
Thank you both from the bottom of my heart!

SOUL JUSTICE

And now, the wonderful ninth soul level! Within it lies the powerful energy of justice. Soul justice also encompasses divine order. It makes perfect sense—when divine justice is restored, divine order naturally follows. And when divine order, the soul's order, is established in your life, a third value comes into play: divine restoration!
Yes, this level holds three sacred forces—justice, order, and restoration.
I can tell you, and you may already feel it—this carries tremendous power. Oh yes, an incredible force is unleashed here!
Always let divine justice work within you, for through it, you call upon divine order in all areas of your life, allowing it to do its best for you.
And the most beautiful part? By doing so, you activate restoration, which means that no matter what has happened—regardless of when soul justice and therefore divine order have fallen out of

balance, whether through your own actions or external influences—it will be restored. And through this, divine restoration takes effect.
Everything that is meant for you will come to you.
Nothing is ever truly lost.
What belongs to you will always find its way back to you.
Isn't that wonderful?
I love this soul level!
I invite you to activate, heal, and recharge it within yourself!
Divine justice now takes effect in my life.
The divine order I call forth brings peace into my being and my world.
I believe in divine restoration.
Maat and Kali are the perfect combination for this, and I can assure you—you will feel their power!

Short Prayer:
My beloved Maat and Kali, you are so powerful, so clear, and the pure embodiment of justice, order, and restoration.
I know that with your divine assistance, these three sacred forces are now fully reactivated, and above all, divine restoration takes place.
The good that has fallen victim to negativity is now instantly restored!
The eternal law of justice and order is now performing its perfect work.
Thank you so much!

SOUL LOYALTY

The tenth soul level is filled with loyalty. Just take a moment to feel the energy of relaxation that soul loyalty creates. Loyalty means consistency, reliability, and above all, connection!
You can probably feel it—these are values that seem to be increasingly rare in the world today. Everything feels unstable and unreliable. The feeling of being connected, completely loved, accepted, and appreciated—has been almost lost.
You can imagine that for most people, this soul level has fallen into scarcity. Has it for you, too?

Take a deep breath and check in with yourself.

Soul loyalty—do you feel it? This wonderful energy that is deeply linked with a sense of profound connection?

Connection to yourself, to all living beings, to the universe, to all souls, angelic beings, and God.

Can you feel the absolute reliability and consistency expanding, filling, and strengthening your entire being?

If this level were reawakened in all people, they would be at absolute peace with themselves, and so would the entire world.

Let's restore, balance, and heal it together.

Deep connection, reliability, and consistency are now growing within me.

Soul loyalty fills my being.

I value myself and can trust in all good things.

Archangel Raguel and Archangel Haniel embody divine loyalty and will assist you in awakening this soul level.

Short Prayer:

My beloved Archangel Raguel and wonderful Archangel Haniel, thank you for standing by my side and restoring balance to my tenth soul level.

I now feel how you fully restore soul loyalty, along with the deep connection and love that come with it.

With this restoration, appreciation, strength, consistency, and reliability unfold naturally within me.

I thank you from the bottom of my heart for your help, and for allowing me to feel my connection to all living beings.

Thank you so much!

SOUL ABUNDANCE

This is the eleventh soul level, where you step into true abundance. The abundance and wealth of the soul reflect the infinite prosperity of the universe. Everything is richly provided, everything is full, everything strives for growth, everything is filled with golden energy, everything is energy!

Both above in the higher realms and here on Earth. Every sound is energy, every word, every meal, every piece of clothing, every banknote, every thought—everything. Now, immerse everything in richness and abundance, and you will walk your soul path and make the most of it. Do not see the Earth as something separate—it is energy, EVERYTHING is energy. So, you can release anything—as above, so below; as below, so above.

Once this truth becomes crystal clear to you, you can finally use your key to happiness.

To assist you in activating this energy flow, Lakshmi and Abundantia are perfect guides!

Short Prayer:
My beloved Lakshmi and Abundantia, a thousand thanks for your help in activating my wealth and abundance. With your divine assistance, I leave behind every state of lack. Everything within and around me now shines in your sparkling, magical energy of prosperity, because I know that everything is energy. Today, I choose to nourish, cultivate, and live only the positive.
With this restoration, all positive wealth energy unfolds, all doors and gates open, and the endless abundance of the universe flows effortlessly toward me!
Thank you so much!

SOUL PROTECTION

This magnificent soul level encompasses safety and, above all, courage. How many people feel insecure? It's no wonder, given the vast amount of shadow creations that have emerged in recent years. So many have lost their courage, but now you know: True security comes from within—from the deep understanding that:
You are profoundly loved. Everything has been prepared for the highest good. You are supported. YOU love YOURSELF so much

that you have already provided yourself with everything good.
You are the most beautiful and radiant being that exists—eternally connected to your Higher Mind, your soul, your Higher Heart, and your divine core—the Over-Soul, embedded in God, safely and continuously sustained.
Wow—isn't that truly empowering?
What else can be said except… WOW!
To strengthen you on this path, Archangel Metatron and Apollo—two fiery, incredibly powerful angelic beings—stand ready to assist you.

Short Prayer:
Beloved Archangel Metatron, you are so strong and protective. I know that the moment I call upon you, you arrive like a force of nature—shielding me and granting me the courage to achieve anything. Together with you, dear Apollo, you create within me a profound sense of security. Because this security is now restored on the soul level, it blossoms from deep within me.
Nothing and no one can ever take it away from me again, and I know that you are always by my side.
Thank you so much!

Your Soul Essence

Feel blessed. You are the blessing in your life. You are the blessing in the lives of others. You are blessed, and blessings fill you.
The soul essence—the unmistakable light within each of us—embodies the deepest truth and purity of our being. It is the eternal core that remains untouched by external circumstances and flows directly from the Source of the Universe. This essence is what makes you unique—your true self beyond all masks and roles.

What Defines the Soul Essence?

Our soul essence is an infinite treasure of love, wisdom, and potential. It carries the memories and experiences not only of this life but of all time and connects us to the higher truths of existence. It is the voice of intuition. It is the inner compass that guides, teaches, and comforts us. It is your unique fingerprint in the vast universe.

The Radiance of the Soul Essence

Like a shining star, our soul essence illuminates the universe.
It attracts what resonates with its light. It connects us with other souls on the deepest level. It weaves a web of light, love, and consciousness. Its radiance gives us the ability to share love and healing, inspiring us to live with authenticity and compassion.

The Value oft he Soul Essence

The value of our soul essence is immeasurable. It is the eternal spark that remains when all things temporary fade. Through its expression, we experience joy, peace, and deep connection with all that is.
In seeking our true self, we uncover the precious quality of our soul essence—the core from which all beauty and creation arise.
By embracing this essence and sharing it with the world, we fulfill our unique place in the cosmic tapestry, enriching the universe with

our individual light. Listen within. Give space to this sacred part of you. Let the symphony of your soul essence resonate in your life. May its light illuminate your path and lead you in a radiant dance of life.

Affirmations to Awaken the Soul

Affirmations are a wonderful way—or rather, a wonderful companion—for every day. Ask your soul to grow ever larger. Ask it to unfold its full energy and play a great role in this world. You are the unique soul—there is only one of you. Only one.
Only YOU can be YOU and gift yourself to this world.
Dream big, dream colorful, dream in abundance!
I wish for you to spread magic—your SOUL MAGIC!
These affirmations come from the soul level and will help you unfold your soul magic from within.
Every time you speak an affirmation, embrace your soul in your thoughts.
Enjoy unfolding your soul magic, and with every spoken affirmation, let your power shine even brighter. Return to the being of the soul.
Every soul must be allowed to be as it truly is and to show its beauty—this is how we fulfill our true life purpose, making our earthly path light, harmonious, and peaceful.

My soul is allowed to BE.

I awaken my soul in the most magical colors

I am the most WONDERFUL and ABUNDANT being that exists.

God is my strength

I am the soul, tender and powerful at the same time

I am the magical soul.

I am my soul and now I experience my soul magic.

My soul magic unfolds and spreads as if by itself.

117

I dream big, I dream colorfully and manifest this through my body in this world.

My soul is my source of strength, so I am always full of energy.

My soul light shines into this world as pure love.

There is peace in my world.

There is joy in my world.

There is love in my world.

I am the purest, divine light of love.

I am loved by my oversoul.

My soul light is infinite, eternal and healthy.

I bring happiness because my soul swims in a sea of happiness.

All my cells are flooded with my soul light.

I love love and love loves me

I see life as THE opportunity to give away love

My soul loves your soul and your soul loves my soul

My higher heart beats in harmony with the cosmic heart and my heart

Everything inside me jumps for joy because there is so much to love

All the love and joy that I give today comes back a millionfold

I am in harmony with EVERYTHING and EVERYONE

I am a wonderful soul and love myself

With my golden canvas in my layout level I only create miracles

My higher mind loves me so much and whispers infinite love to me

My soul radiates warmth and love

All relationships in my life are harmonious and fulfilling

I breathe in and out soul dust

The wisdom of my soul is now unfolding
My soul light shines like the sun and fills everything in my life
I love myself and my heart overflows with this love

My soul shines

Wisdom and spiritual intelligence are a pulsating energy in my life

I love my life, myself, my family and my friends and they love me

I was born to love and be loved

I am the good

My blueprint has all the tools I need to be successful

I am the power of the good in my soul

My soul is my source of strength

Perfect soul love is present in abundance, in every moment

I love my soul and my soul loves me

My heart is wide open and thus my soul radiates through it into the world

I always find love, no matter where I am or what I do, because we souls are always connected.

At my side, EVERYONE grows

I am rich, all wealth is already in my soul.

In my subconscious there is a wonderful team of cheerleaders who cheer me on, build me up and celebrate

I am rich in soul energy

Miracles now follow miracles

One soul miracle after another is now unfolding in my life

I know that whatever happens is for my best

I forgive everyone who has ever hurt me, because my soul forgives their soul and their soul forgives my soul

My soul unfolds more and more every day

My magical consciousness is in close connection with my Higher Mind

Life loves me

My soul's shine fills everything, no matter where I go

The shine of my soul is my greatest protection

My soul's path now blossoms right in front of me in golden light

I walk my path with confidence, because I know that EVERYTHING that belongs to me now comes to me. Simple, easy, because it finds me

Divine redemption is now in effect and all that is meant for me is now coming to me, from all directions of time

My soul is leaping with joy and delight

My soul is playing a major role

My soul is now unfolding every miracle in my life

My soul is a shining beacon of light guiding me to my highest potential.

I trust in the wisdom and guidance of my soul to lead me on the right path.

I am connected to the infinite power of the universe and my soul is the channel for this divine, universal energy.

I embrace the unique gifts and talents that lie within my soul and share them with the world with gratitude and joy.

I am such a powerful co-creator and I now manifest all of my true soul desires in the magic of my soul light.

My soul is indestructible and fully equipped and capable of mastering any challenges that present themselves to me. I honor the sacredness of my soul journey and trust in divine timing.

From the depths of my magical soul, I radiate love, compassion and kindness that touches the lives of others.

I am worthy of receiving all of the blessings and indescribable abundance that the universe has in store for me.

I am a divine being of light and my soul's purpose is to shine brightly and leave a positive impression on the world.

My soul is an endless source of love, compassion, joy and lightness and I share my light with all living beings.

I trust my divine soul plan that unfolds before me, with the certainty of fulfilling my soul potential.

I now let go of my limiting beliefs and embrace all my new, infinite possibilities that rise from the depths of my soul.

I am a chalice of divine wisdom and I allow divine guidance to illuminate my soul path.

I now honor and nourish my soul with self-love, self-worth, self-confidence and self-respect and thereby also my fellow human beings with compassion, empathy and love.

I am in a wonderful connection with the collective soul consciousness and I know that my soul light serves the healing and transformation of all.

I am a magnet for positive energy and positive experiences and attract only the highest and best for my soul.
I believe in the natural power of my soul to be able to heal and restore everything in all areas of my life.

I am worthy of receiving all the love, abundance and blessings that the universe has in store for me.

I bless my soul journey and my growth, knowing that my soul evolution is truly a sacred, protected and magical process.

Please always remember that affirmations are effective when you repeat them often, with all your enthusiasm, and especially with all your soul love.
Choose the affirmation every day that resonates most with your soul.
Let the affirmations serve as a constant reminder of your true being - your soul.

Write down your own affirmations:

The Magic of Released Soul Essence

When you lift the veil of shadow creations and release your soul essence in all its splendor, a beautiful dance of transformation begins. This essence is the pure expression of your true nature—indestructible, eternal, and full of light. Once it unfolds, it becomes a source of infinite possibilities, touching and illuminating every aspect of your life.

The joy of living your soul is an incomparable and profound experience. It feels like finally coming home after a long search—to the harbor of your true essence. When you live from the joy of your soul, you experience fulfillment beyond the ordinary—a joy that arises from the deep connection with your own truth and the universe.

By embracing your full potential, you open the doors to a world of wonder and magic. Every decision, every action is carried by clarity and authenticity. You have become the architect of your own reality. Aura architecture is no longer foreign to you, you have learned to direct, utilize, and create with your energy. I wish for your golden canvas to have become an integral part of your life, one you use daily so that harmony and fulfillment spread into your everyday experiences. Your heart pulses in rhythm with the universe, and everything you do is infused with meaning and joy. Through your third eye, you once again gaze into the light, into the magnificent realms of consciousness. You hear the loving voice of your Higher Mind once more, your subconscious cheerleader team can celebrate you, and much more. You will perceive many positive and miraculous changes in various areas of your life.

When you give your soul the space to express itself, the magic of life begins to unfold. You attract experiences and people who resonate with your true self, nurturing your growth and joy. Creativity flows through you, and you discover new ways to express your uniqueness.

Positive Effects in Life Areas:

1) Finances/Money:
- By releasing your soul essence, you attract abundance and prosperity. Money is energy—when you free your true energy, you also unlock your financial energy. You deserve abundance and wealth. You will witness a miraculous transformation in this area, with new opportunities to create and share prosperity becoming visible, allowing you to be generous in both giving and receiving.
- The concept of money as an energy flow teaches us that wealth is not only measured in material possessions but also in the freedom and abundance we create in our lives. When you begin to release your inner energy and shine in all its facets, you invite this natural flow of abundance and opportunities into your life.
- Once you understand financial wealth as a form of energy, the idea of lack loses its significance. You realize that it is about raising your frequency and letting go of inner resistance that blocks the natural flow.

2) Relationships:
- In relationships, the pure integrity and honesty of your essence flourish. You communicate clearly and with an open heart, fostering deep, trusting connections. You attract people into your life who share your values, and together, you celebrate the miracle of love and mutual growth.
- With this deep, intimate relationship with yourself, the vibration of your entire being changes. You radiate authenticity and self-confidence that are irresistible. The love you give yourself now also attracts love from the outside—love that is true and fulfilling. This growing self-love unfolds like a flower and catches the universe's attention.
- In the flow of this energy, a wonderful romantic relationship may enter your life, or your existing one will improve

126

significantly. A connection that nourishes and enriches your soul, based on mutual appreciation, joy, and support. This relationship reflects the love you have cultivated within yourself and offers you the opportunity to share it with a special person.

3) Family:

- Within your family, you enhance harmony and support. Your authentic presence inspires your loved ones to unfold their own souls. An atmosphere of acceptance and unconditional understanding emerges, where everyone is encouraged to live their own truth.
- **Self-Worth:** Allow yourself to recognize and celebrate your own value. This attracts positive energy in the form of opportunities and appreciation. The greatest gift you can give to another is to take care of yourself and trust that they, too, can take care of themselves.
- **Gratitude:** Practice gratitude for what is already in your life and for every single person around you. This opens the door to a richer flow, dispelling thoughts of lack and helping you see how deeply loved you are.
- **Giving and Receiving:** Find balance in giving and receiving to promote and enjoy the energy flow. When you give without expectation, you create a channel that also allows for receiving. Miracles happen within your family.
- **Focus:** Direct your energy toward projects that inspire and excite you. Your genuine enthusiasm will create a powerful vortex of creative expression and abundance, uplifting your entire family.

4) Career:

- In your professional life, you navigate with clarity and determination. Your talents and abilities flow effortlessly, and you find fulfillment in work that aligns with your soul mission. You are recognized as a natural leader and innovator, inspiring others through positivity and vision.

- The moment you begin living with passion and enthusiasm, you step into a creative energy that influences everything around you. You attract opportunities and people who resonate with your energy, fostering growth and fulfillment in all aspects of your life and experiencing a synchronicity that enriches your daily existence. ALL DOORS OPEN.
- The key lies in listening to the whispers of your heart and finding the courage to follow this inner guidance. By embracing life with an open heart, you realize that your life's purpose is not a distant goal but a path that unfolds with every step taken in joy and love.

5) Health:

- The new energy, joy, peace, and fully expanded soul essence can have profound positive effects on your health. When you live from a space of inner harmony and enthusiasm, it not only enhances your mental and emotional well-being but also significantly benefits your physical health—because everything is frequency!
- Strengthened Immune System: Joy and inner peace promote the release of positive neurotransmitters and hormones such as serotonin and dopamine, which strengthen the immune system, increase resilience to illnesses, and improve overall health.

  ○ Reduced Stress: When you live in harmony with your soul essence, your stress levels decrease significantly. This leads to a lower release of stress hormones like cortisol, reducing the risk of stress-related illnesses.

  ○ Improved Emotional Health: The joy and peace you experience contribute to a more stable emotional state. Emotional balance can alleviate depression and anxiety, leading to better mental health.

○ Increased Energy and Vitality: Your new vibrational energy gives you a sense of vitality and drive, invigorating your entire body. With more energy, you achieve your health goals more easily and feel overall more comfortable and alive.

○ Better Sleep Quality: Peace and joy promote restful, deep sleep. A well-rested body regenerates more effectively, leading to better health and cellular repair.

○ Encouragement of Healthy Habits: When your mind is positively attuned and you are rooted in your soul essence, you are more likely to make healthy choices—whether in nutrition, exercise, or social well-being.

○ Mind-Body Connection: Your soul essence strengthens the connection between mind and body. This unity helps reduce physical ailments and promotes overall well-being.

When you embrace the magic of your soul essence and live your full potential, you create a life full of wonder and fulfillment. You are meant to share your uniqueness with the world—by showing your true colors and expressing your truth. The more you do this, the more you become a beacon of authenticity, inspiring others to do the same. In connection with your soul, you find an unshakable peace that supports you through life's challenges. You know that deep within, you have the resilience to overcome any difficulty with grace and wisdom. This inner peace brings forth a joy that is not dependent on external circumstances but is rooted in your very being.
May this journey bring you love, joy, peace, and a deep connection with the world around you. May your enthusiasm be a powerful energy source, fueling you with motivation and perseverance, driving you to explore new horizons and experience life in all its fullness.

Be a Leader

We have reached the end of my book. You have resolved so much and gained many tools to ensure that you never again get caught in the creations of shadows.

But now it's time to take action—bring it into the present, into reality. Think like a millionaire, act with strength and perseverance, be the star of your life, and a blessing to the world. You are a leader, with a healed heart, manifesting your visions in the world!

A healthy mindset is the key to being truly successful and achieving greatness in this world. It all begins with the belief that you have the power to shape your life actively and create something positive. This mindset paves the way for outstanding success and the fulfillment of your boldest dreams.

Imagine starting each day with a clear vision and an unshakable belief in your abilities. You don't see obstacles as insurmountable barriers but as opportunities for growth, as stepping stones to new possibilities, knowing that something beautiful always emerges from everything. With this attitude, you attract opportunities and navigate every challenge with confidence and determination.

Success is not just about reaching a goal; it is also about the journey itself. With a strong mindset, you prepare yourself to give your best in every moment and learn from every mistake. You become more resilient, flexible, and creative—qualities that truly make you stand out.

When you combine this inner alignment with passion and consistent effort, you will not only experience success but also serve as a beacon of inspiration for others. Be a leader, and know that your dedication and authenticity have the power to initiate profound change in the world. You can uplift communities, foster innovation, and make a real difference in people's lives.

Set ambitious goals, cultivate a proactive perspective, and surround yourself with supportive people. With a strong mindset, you are well-equipped to be not only successful but extraordinary. The world is waiting for what you have to offer—go out and leave your unforgettable mark!

At the end of this journey, you now stand with a heart full of insights and a soul ready to step into the world. Everything you have learned and resolved so far is a valuable foundation—but now it's truly time to put all this knowledge into action. Leave behind the shadow creations of the past and focus on the powerful present.

Start thinking like a millionaire, full of confidence and visionary foresight. Act with the strength and perseverance of a leader who knows their purpose and is ready to live it. Be the star of your own life, illuminating your path with the clarity and courage that you carry within. Your healed heart is the source of infinite possibilities and deep compassion.

You are not just a part of this world—you are a blessing to it. Your visions are unique and meaningful, and the world is waiting for you to manifest them. Use your inner strength and turn your dreams into reality. Move forward, inspire others, and create a world of light and love through your actions and your being.

Now the time has come. The stage is yours. Bring your dreams to life and experience the magic that unfolds when passion becomes reality. You are ready to enrich the world with your radiant light.

Acknowledgment

My dear reader,

I write these final lines of my book with a heart filled with gratitude and deep appreciation for you. You have embarked on this journey to your soul with me, and your presence and dedication mean the world to me!
I feel truly honored that you have shared the sacredness of your soul with me. Thank you for opening your heart and soul to the wisdom and insights within these pages. My deepest wish is that I have touched your soul, inspired you, and provided you with guidance for your own soul's path—toward growth and expansion.
Your commitment to personal transformation and your determination to read this book to the very end should make you proud. It is a testament to your courage! Hearing the call of your soul and embarking on the journey of self-reflection is a sign of inner strength and a profound desire to live your full potential.
Please know that YOUR journey does not end with the last lines of this book—it is only just beginning!
Integrate what you have learned into your daily life, share it with the world. Enchant the souls around you and trust in the power of your own soul!
People can tell you many things, but now you know—EVERYTHING LIES WITHIN YOU!
You are a magnificent composition of your soul's essence, your HIGHER SELF. Within it rests your HIGHER HEART, which is in direct connection with the cosmic heart and your own heart.
Deeply connected comes your INDIVIDUAL SOUL, united with your HIGHER MIND, which branches into your LAYOUT LEVEL and your BLUEPRINT.
Then emerges a composition for the entire world—the MASS COLLECTIVE—transitioning into your INDIVIDUAL LEVEL, which gently flows into your SUBCONSCIOUS MIND, before it enters your CONSCIOUS MIND and PHYSICAL MIND, where it transforms into

a perfect symphony—expressing the true essence of YOU.

You are whole and complete!

On your soul's journey, you can always return to this book whenever you need guidance, or feel free to reach out to me in any way!

Always remember, YOU ARE NOT ALONE!

You will perceive the magic of souls, recognize all your guides and helpers, and who knows—perhaps a new, enchanting soul is waiting to cross your path.

Then you will know that the universe is always FOR you, and most importantly, from today onward, your soul will guide you with its ancient wisdom! Trust the whispers of your heart, for you know it is the voice of your soul, protected and guided by your Higher Mind.

You will walk your soul's path with certainty, a path prepared just for you, filled with joy, magic, and miracles!

To conclude, I would love to gift you my favorite affirmation. I cherish it because it reflects infinite trust in the levels of consciousness, in God, in the Higher Self, the Higher Mind, and all the wonderful helpers around us:

"There is golden dust in the air for me. Through my determined, clear, and affirmative thinking, I now begin to absorb this golden dust, and from this very moment, I start to experience golden dust results!"

From the depths of my heart—thank you! And with that, my soul kisses your soul.

With deep love,
Yours,
Nadine

Contact details:

Website:
www.nadinesimmerock.com

Instagram:
@nadine_simmerock

YouTube channel to practice my meditations (German, English, and Spanish versions) and to listen to my podcasts:
@NadineSimmerock

Enjoy everything!
Yours Nadine